QUALITATIVE UTILITARIANISM

Daniel Holbrook

UNIVERSITY
PRESS OF
AMERICA

Lanham • New York • London

Copyright © **1988 by**

University Press of America,® Inc.

4720 Boston Way
Lanham, MD 20706

3 Henrietta Street
London WC2E 8LU England

All rights reserved

Printed in the United States of America

British Cataloging in Publication Information Available

ISBN 0–8191–6989–7 (pbk. : alk. paper)
ISBN 0–8191–6988–9 (alk. paper)

All University Press of America books are produced on acid-free paper which exceeds the minimum standards set by the National Historical Publications and Records Commission.

QUALITATIVE UTILITARIANISM
TABLE OF CONTENTS

INTRODUCTION.. 1

CHAPTER ONE: CONSEQUENTIALISM

    1. The Definition of Consequentialism........ 5
    2. `Right´ and `Ought´....................... 13
    3. An Analysis of Freedom.................... 19
    4. General Consequentialism.................. 27
    5. The Paradox of Consequentialism........... 34
    6. Act and Rule Consequentialism............. 36
    7. A Final Rejoinder......................... 40

CHAPTER TWO: HEDONISM

    1. Hedonism and Humanism..................... 41
    2. Psychological Hedonism.................... 44
    3. Ethical Hedonism.......................... 51
    4. The Sensation Theory of Pleasure.......... 55
    5. Pleasure and Desire....................... 60

CHAPTER THREE: QUALITATIVE HEDONISM

    1. Quantitative Hedonism..................... 69
    2. Critique of Quantitative Utilitarianism... 74
    3. Qualitative Hedonism...................... 81
    4. The Charge of Inconsistency............... 83
    5. The Epistemology of Qualitative Hedonism.. 90
    6. Pluralistic Qualitative Hedonism.......... 101
    7. Pleasure and Happiness.................... 105

CHAPTER FOUR: QUALITATIVE UTILITARIANISM

    1. The Definition of the Theory.............. 109
    2. The Proof of the Theory................... 111
    3. Utilitarianism and the Individual......... 121
    4. Practical Implications of the Theory...... 128
    5. Concluding Remarks........................ 131

BIBLIOGRAPHY.. 133

INDEX... 137

INTRODUCTION

Both Plato and Aristotle placed great value on the pleasures associated with intellectual activity. In the <u>Republic</u> (587b-e), Plato offers a proof that a philosopher king leads a life 729 times more pleasant than a dictator who has all he desires, but lacks wisdom. Similarly, Aristotle argues in <u>Nicomachean Ethics</u> (Book X, Chapter 8) for the superiority of the pleasures that accompany a life of contemplation.

This book is about an ethical theory with the name `Qualitative Utilitarianism´. This theory was first put forth in detail by John Stuart Mill in his well-known essay <u>Utilitarianism</u>. What makes this theory unique is that distinctions between various qualities of pleasure, similar to those made by Plato and Aristotle, are incorporated within a utilitarian framework.

I shall begin with Mill´s definition of utilitarianism, and after that, examine how he incorporates qualitative distinctions of pleasure within it. Mill´s definition is:

> The creed which accepts as the foundation of morals "utility" or the "greatest happiness principle" holds that actions are right in proportion as they tend to promote happiness; wrong as they tend to produce the reverse of happiness. By happiness is intended pleasure and the absence of pain; by unhappiness, pain and the privation of pleasure.(<u>Utilitarianism</u>, p. 7)

There are two distinct concepts within this definition. Mill writes, "actions are right as they tend to promote happiness", which I understand to mean, FIRST, it is for the reason of what they promote (their effects) that actions are right or wrong, and SECOND, the production of pleasure and pain are the only effects that count towards an action´s being right or wrong. So, what Mill defines as `utilitarianism´ is more precisely `hedonistic consequentialism´.

Two paragraphs further into <u>Utilitarianism</u>, Mill rejects a purely quantitative system as a method to evaluate pleasure. The rejection of the Benthamite quantitative method leads to Mill´s view that there are

INTRODUCTION

qualitative distinctions in the evaluation of pleasure. He writes:

> It is quite compatible with the principle of utility to recognize the fact that some kinds of pleasure are more desirable and more valuable than others. It would be absurd that...the estimation of pleasure should be supposed to depend on quantity alone. (<u>Utilitarianism</u>, p. 8)

Here, Mill is clearly saying that to limit oneself to a purely quantitative theory in the evaluation of pleasure leads to absurdity. A quantitative theory defines the value of pleasure as solely being determined by the quantity of pleasure present in some experience. Quantitative Hedonism is based upon the assumption that pleasure is a simple, homogeneous quality that lends itself to quantification. Qualitative Hedonism is defined negatively as being any version of hedonism that is not quantitative. These two theories will be further examined and compared in the third chapter of this book.

Mill, in effect, defines utilitarianism as hedonistic consequentialism. In the twentieth century, utilitarianism is often identified with consequentialism, which allows for non-hedonistic versions of utilitarianism. For example, J.J.C. Smart begins his "Extreme and Restricted Utilitarianism"(1956) (p. 171) with the definition:

> Utilitarianism is the doctrine that the rightness and wrongness of actions is to be judged by their consequences.

Henry Sidgwick in <u>The Methods of Ethics</u> (1874) (p. 84) defines utilitarianism as "universalistic hedonism". Thus, with the turn of the century, the meaning of `utilitarianism´ has seemingly changed from hedonistic consequentialism to consequentialism, whatever its form. However, this change in meaning has not been universally adopted. Some recent works, Narveson´s <u>Morality and Utility</u> (p. 14), for example, still identify utilitarianism with hedonistic utilitarianism. In the preface of <u>Utilitarian Ethics</u>, Anthony Quinton claims that the ethics of Mill and Bentham are the

INTRODUCTION

paradigms of utilitarianism. There are non-hedonistic utilitarianisms, for example, the the Ideal Utilitarianism of G.E. Moore's Principia Ethica (pp. 183-225).

The root of the word `utilitarianism´ is `utility´, meaning `usefullness´. The view of the early utilitarians was that only pleasure (and/or happiness) has intrinsic value and that things other than pleasure have utility only if they are a means towards the production of pleasure. Non-hedonistic versions of utilitarianism are founded upon denying that only pleasure has intrinsic value, which leads to denying that only the means to pleasure have `utility´. Hedonism does not seem to be implied by the meaning of `utilitarianism´. But for sake of brevity, what I shall be calling `Qualitative Utilitarianism´ is more precisely, `Qualitatively-Hedonistic Utilitarianism.´

Qualitative Utilitarianism is thus defined as the theory that actions are right or wrong on account of the pleasure and pain that result from them, and that the evaluation of pleasure is a complex matter, involving qualitative distinctions, and is not merely the quantification of a single, homogeneous quality.

I will be defending the thesis that Qualitative Utilitarianism is a respectable and sound moral theory (though, not necessarily the only respectable and sound moral theory). Until recent times, the theory has not generally been held in high esteem. The purpose of this essay is to further define and examine the theory, defend it, and describe its practical applications.

Qualitative Utilitarianism is based upon two separate theories, consequentialism and qualitative hedonism. The organization of the following .four chapters follows the development of these two theories into Qualitative Utilitarianism. The title of Chapter One is "Consequentialism", and Chapters Two and Three are titled "Hedonism" and "Qualitative Hedonism". In Chapter Four, "Qualitative Utilitarianism", both of these theories are combined, and the practical applications of the combined theories are examined.

I should say that, although I see Mill as being the first and foremost proponent of Qualitative Utilitarianism, this is not intended to be the type of essay that attempts to bring together the various parts

INTRODUCTION

of his ethical philosophy into a coherent whole. I will comment on connections between the ethics of <u>Utilitarianism</u> and Mill's other works, but I do not intend to explain or defend all of the aspects of Mill's theory. My interest is primarily in the Qualitative Utilitarianism theory itself. Mill's essay is a brilliant, but incomplete, statement of the theory. I have found no other work on Qualitative Utilitarianism that defends and explains the theory in any great detail. That is why I have chosen to write this essay.

CHAPTER ONE

CONSEQUENTIALISM

1. THE DEFINITION OF CONSEQUENTIALISM

I begin with the following four assumptions: FIRST, there exist actions, that is, things that we do that have an impact on world events. SECOND, there exist events when there are several alternative actions open to us, any one of which might become actual. THIRD, Each of these alternative actions, if performed, has an effect on world events distinct from the effects of the other alternatives. FOURTH, we are often free to choose, perform, and realize the effects of one action to the exclusion of its alternatives. AND FIFTH, only real actions have real effects

Consequentialism is a method of evaluating actions in respect to their being right or wrong. According to consequentialism, what is relevant to a particular action being right or wrong is only its actual effects or, in other words, its "consequences". A general type of action is evaluated by looking at all of the consequences of the particular actions that fall under the more general category.

Consequentialism directs our attention to actual effects of an action. It does not tell us what effects are better than others. This subject is covered later in Chapters Two and Three.

I am defining consequentialism to be the theory that actions are right or wrong solely on account of their actual effects. So, non-consequentialists hold that something other than its actual effects is relevant to an action's being right or wrong. Other forms of non-consequentialism claim that the motive that precedes an action, or maybe, the rule an action falls under, or even, simply the kind of action it is, is relevant to an action's being right or wrong.

A different version of consequentialism from that which I am defining here claims an action is right only if the effects that most reasonably could be expected to follow from it produces the maximum benefits. I don't see this as really being consequentialism in respect to the evaluation of particular actions because it confuses the effects of an action with the motive or epistemic state of the agent, and keeping these issues

THE DEFINITION OF CONSEQUENTIALISM

separate is (as I see it) important if a clear and accurate account of consequentialism is to be given. No particular action has a probable effect. Rather, an agent believes that an action will probably have the effect he or she has in mind. To say that an action is right only if the agent could reasonably expect it to result in maximum benefits is not what I mean by consequentialism, since this would place the evaluation of the action primarily on the agent's motive or epistemic state. I assume that only real actions have real effects. So, by consequentialism, I mean that each real action is to be evaluated on account of its actual consequences. Types of actions have probable effects based on the actual effects of the actions that fall under that type. To hold that it is right to undertake a particular action for the reason that this type of action regularly produces good consequences is a view that relies on observation of consequences but is not consequentialism in respect to that particular action. The epistemic state of the agent is relevant to how he decides what action to perform, not whether or not the action itself is right. I shall return to this topic shortly (p. 19) in distinguishing between a right action and an action one ought to perform.

Consequentialism should not be confused with the idea that "the end justifies the means", if this phrase means that only the realization of some final state of affairs is relevant to an action's being right or wrong, with no weight placed on the intervening events. A consequentialist is not solely interested in the end result, Instead, all of the effects of an action are counted. "The end justifies the means" doctrine compares to sailing from England to Boston solely for the reason of arriving there, as was true in the case of the Pilgrims. Consequentialism compares more closely to those who sail solo across the Atlantic for the adventure of it. For them, the end of the voyage is not the main reason behind their actions, and instead, they are aiming for the effects of the entire journey.(1)

---

1. This point is made on pp. 83-84 in Bernard Williams' "A critique of utilitarianism" (see bibliography for complete reference information), and also on pp. 503-505 in Anne Stubbs' "The Pros and Cons of Consequentialism".

THE DEFINITION OF CONSEQUENTIALISM

According to consequentialism, the value of an action is not determined by its intrinsic qualities, but rather by its actual effects. The intrinsic qualities of an action are those qualities that place the action within a general category. One type of intrinsic quality includes those qualities that differentiate a verbal action from one that is ambulatory. Generally, the intrinsic qualities of an action are the more important characteristics of an action, excepting its causal properties.

There are three general temporal areas that figure in the analysis of an action. FIRST, there are the events prior to the performance of the action, the most important being the psychological properties of the agent that lead to his or her decision to act in some particular way. SECOND, there is the performance of the action, most often executed through motion of the body, whether it be uttering a sentence or something less subtle, such as striking an assailant. AND THIRD, there are the effects that occur after the action has been performed. These distinctions are often blurred, but do hold for the majority of actions. A pianist contemplates his performance while he is playing. There is often no clear line between teaching a class and the effects that follow.

For the purposes of making an ethical evaluation, consequentialism separates the psychological properties of the agent from the performance of the action and the causal properties that follow. Consequentialism also separates the intrinsic properties of the action from its effects, both those that occur during the performance of the action and those that follow later. To hold consequentialism is to hold that only the actual effects of an action are relevant in its ethical evaluation. The agent´s motivation usually occurs prior to the performance of the action, so it is not an effect of the action, and so, is a matter held by consequentialists to be separate from the evaluation of the action itself. The intrinsic properties of the action are also not effects of the action, and so are also held by consequentialists not to be relevant in the ethical evaluation of the action.

Two intrinsically similar actions can have extremely dissimilar effects. For example, two boys can spend the afternoon together shooting at any movement

THE DEFINITION OF CONSEQUENTIALISM

in the forest. One boy hits only brush, but the second boy wounds a deer and a hiker. Within the context of ethical evaluation, a consequentialist would hold the actions of the two boys to be very different, since they have dissimilar effects. The motivation was similar, and both boys deserve censure for being careless. Whether the bullet hits a stump or a human being, the act of pointing a gun towards movement in the brush is intrinsically no different, although aiming at a human being differs intrinsically from aiming at a stump. In the case at hand, wounding a human is an event that occurs after the action of aiming a gun and pulling the trigger. According to consequentialism, only the effects of an action are important in its ethical evaluation. The actions of the two boys had very different effects. The second boy´s actions were very "wrong" because of their undesirable effects.

Theories opposed to consequentialism evaluate actions by criteria other than their actual effects. One opposing theory is to hold that an action can be evaluated simply by looking at its intrinsic properties. An example of this position is the view put forth by Anne Stubbs in "The Pros and Cons of Consequentialism" (p. 503). There she writes about a case of embezzlement on the part of an employee of a financial institution:

> ...it is possible to condemn this action, not on the grounds of its consequences, which need not even be known, but on the ground of its being an instance of theft and therefore <u>dishonest</u>.

When Stubbs writes, "it is possible to condemn this action", I assume that she means that it is reasonable to condemn the action without knowledge of the effects of that particular action. To defend consequentialism, I reply that, as a class, dishonest actions deserve censure because they generally produce undesirable effects, but that without knowing its effects, a particular action cannot be completely evaluated. It is possible that this act of theft has the effect of saving thousands of lives, and if Stubbs values human life more than she disdains dishonest actions then she must alter her position. I think that, in the final analysis, Stubbs is not condemning this particular

THE DEFINITION OF CONSEQUENTIALISM

action but is condemning dishonest actions in general, a position consistent with consequentialism. That is not to say that Stubbs must become a consequentialist, if she is to be consistent, for her view more likely is that unless the dishonest act has overwhelmingly beneficial effects, the action should be condemned. Any plausible position in regard to evaluating particular actions must make some allowance for the actual effects of the action, and thus, the effects of a particular action need to be known, if it is reasonably to be condemned.

We know that theft generally produces harmful effects. Stubbs's position is not that probably this action deserves condemnation, a more easily defended position. Instead, her reasoning seems to be based on the syllogism:

All acts of theft deserve condemnation.
This action is theft.

Therefore, this action deserves condemnation.

This reasoning is inconsistent with consequentialism as herein defined, because it does not place the ethical evaluation of an action on its particular effects. Some instances of theft do produce good consequences, all things considered, and therefore, consequentialists deny the major premise. They claim that it is false that <u>all</u> acts of theft deserve condemnation.

To further illustrate the distinction between consequentialist and non-consequentialist theories, consider the following example: Smith made a large donation that helped a religious organization to establish a colony in South America. Since the colony had the stated purpose of providing a home to displaced persons, Smith's motive was noble, because it was based on a sense of duty to help those in need. Imagine that Smith had good reasons to believe that his action would have good consequences, but in fact things turned out badly, and the action had the worst possible consequences. The leader of the colony was a fanatic who led its members to mass suicide. Would you say that Smith's action was right or wrong? In respect to Smith's motive and from what could reasonably be expected to be the effects of such an action, you might say that the action was right, but in respect to its actual effects,

THE DEFINITION OF CONSEQUENTIALISM

you probably would say that the action was wrong. It is inconsistent to hold that the action itself is both right and wrong.

The consequentialistic solution to the problem is to make distinctions between the ethical properties of the agent, the type of action performed, and the particular action performed. Smith deserves moral credit for trying to do the right thing. Acts of charity generally produce good consequences. But, because of its undesirable effect, Smith's action was wrong. Sometimes in conversation we say things like, "It was unfortunate that things worked out so badly, but Smith was still right in making the donation", which suggests that the `right action´ is not identical to the action that is productive of the best consequences. An explanation that is consistent with consequentialism is that we are reluctant to say that Smith was wrong, for the reason that the actions of people with similar motives and action of this type generally produce good consequences. Smith deserves praise and moral credit for trying to do the right thing, but the consequentialist cannot praise the action itself, for as understood consequentialistically, Smith's action was wrong.

In opposition to the view that there is a clear-cut distinction between the motivation of an agent and the ethical evaluation of his or her action, I again refer to "The Pros and Cons of Consequentialism" (p. 514):

> Consider the following adjectives: selfish; cowardly; benevolent; malevolent; generous; deceitful. They all, I submit, characterize actions in moral terms, they indicate specific ways of acting well or badly. Furthermore, in each case it is a necessary condition of an action's being truly so characterizable <u>that the agent should have a certain reason for what he does</u>...a soldier who leaves the battlefield is not acting in a cowardly way unless he does so through fear of injury or death...

I understand the implied conclusion of the above argument to be that consequentialists are inconsistent

THE DEFINITION OF CONSEQUENTIALISM

because they are committed to the view that an action can be evaluated independently of the motivation that precedes or accompanies it, and Stubbs is saying that this is not possible.

I agree with Stubbs that to judge an action as being `cowardly´ requires reference to the motivation of the agent, and that to employ the adverb `cowardly´ involves making an ethical judgment. We do say, "The soldier fled the battlefield <u>cowardly</u>." Because `cowardly´ is an adverb, the grammatical indication is that the qualification of being cowardly is being applied to the verb `fled´ and not the subject `the soldier´. An important theme in twentieth century philosophy is that grammatical structures are in some cases instructive and in other cases misleading. The lesson to be learned is to be clear about exactly to what we are assenting when we assert a proposition. The assertion `the soldier fled the battlefield cowardly´ is made in the context of war. It describes a person whose occupation is that of a soldier, with the presumption that a soldier often has the duty to stand his ground and not retreat in battle. A soldier can be overcome by fear or place his self-interest over his duty and act cowardly by deserting his post and fleeing dangers of battle.

The grammatical indication that `cowardly´ applies to the action apart from the agent is misleading because it resembles propositions like `the soldier fled the battle stealthily.´ In the latter case, the adverb clearly does apply only to the action because it describes the motions of the soldier. He is moving in a cautious, secretive manner. In the case of a cowardly action, there is no such property of the action, taken in itself, that constitutes cowardice. It is true that cowards often turn and run in some disorderly pattern or try to sneak away undetected. But a crafty coward will turn away from the battle marching as if he is on a special mission or delivering a message, so as not to arouse suspicion. The point is that, in both cases, an adverb modifies a verb that describes an action, but in cases of cowardice, there need not be any quality of that action, taken in itself, that indicates cowardice. In cases of stealth, an action is performed stealthily only if it has certain properties that indicate stealth. Therefore, a clarification is `the soldier, for cowardly reasons, fled the battlefield.´ The same

THE DEFINITION OF CONSEQUENTIALISM

kind of absorption, on the part of the subject, of the quality denoted by the adverb does not happen in cases of stealth. It does not clarify to say `the soldier, for reasons of stealth, fled the battlefield.´ The objection fails once the misleading grammatical structure is clarified.

To generalize, if what we are asserting by using an adverb in a sentence of the form, `a acted x-ly´, cannot be accounted for by an examination of the intrinsic or causal properties of the action, then we may assume that the adverb modifies the subject. In cases of using an adverb with normative content, if the normative content refers indirectly to the motivation of the subject then the normative sense can be absorbed by the subject and be separated from the verb. What follows is that we may use adverbs in our descriptions of actions, and make ethical judgments in doing so, without being committed to the thesis that these judgments are made about actions apart from their consequences, for they are really judgments that pertain to the motivation of the subjects.

From the consequentialistic point of view, making an ethical judgment of an action is essentially a matter of estimating the overall effect it has or would have on world events. In the case of the soldier fleeing from battle, its effects could range from losing the battle, and eventually the war, to something entirely insignificant. It could be that our soldier drove a tank in the Panzer Corps, and that his cowardly act resulted in Moscow being saved, and the Allies´ winning World War II, presumably the alternative with best effects possible. As a consequentialist, I am holding that, in this case, his "cowardly" action was right. Thus, in the ethical evaluation of the action, I can continue to distinguish between the motivation and the effects. In the above example, the condemnation of the action as being cowardly points solely to the agent´s motive and the judgment of the action being `right´ points solely to its effects. It is a case in which the right action is being performed by a cowardly Nazi.

When a consequentialist condemns an action as being cowardly, he or she is pointing towards the agent and his motivation as being cowardly. In fact, what other sense could there be in saying that an <u>action</u> is cowardly? The charge of inconsistency is based on the assumption that the ethical judgment implied by asserting that an action was `cowardly´ commits a consequentialist to making a negative moral judgment on the action apart from its effects, which is inconsistent. But, a consequentialist is perfectly consistent in holding that an action can be both cowardly and right, once everything is made clear, and thus, the objection fails.

2. RIGHT AND OUGHT

Although I am defending consequentialism, I am not claiming that consequentialism is true by definition. That seems to be the view of G.E. Moore when, in Principia Ethica, he writes (2):

> ...to assert that a certain line of conduct is...right...is obviously to assert that more good or less evil will exist in the world, if it be adopted than if anything else be done instead...(p. 25)

> ...the assertion `I am morally bound to perform this action´ is identical with the assertion `This action will produce the greatest possible amount of good in the Universe´...(p. 147)

If it were that simple then it would be hard to explain why intelligent philosophers like Alan Donagan (See Chapter 6 of The Theory of Morality) argue against consequentialism. I think they are mistaken, but I am sure that the reason is not that non-consequentialists have failed to grasp the meaning of `right´. If a person has sufficient experience in using a language then it is highly unlikely that he or she will be confused about the meaning of its most basic terms. `Right´ is an important and a generally well-known word

---

2. Moore seems to be less emphatic on this point in his later work, Ethics. There, he argues that actions are right or wrong according to their actual consequences by showing that any other view leads to paradoxical implications.

in the English language. A person who knows the meaning of `right´ would not, according to Moore´s thinking, be confused by the example of Smith´s donation, with its noble motive and unforseen consequences. Most people do find such examples confusing. Thus, `right´ does not obviously have as its meaning, `cause of the best result´, and thus, Moore is mistaken.

For instance, in one variation of Christian Ethics, a right action is by definition one that complies with God´s Will. Even if Christians believe that all actions that are in accordance with God´s Will always lead to the best consequences, should God change his mind then action in accordance with His Will would still be right even if less than the best consequences followed. I don´t agree, but the disagreement surely isn´t about the meaning of the word `right´. I hold that the meaning of `right´ depends on other assumptions made about the nature of the world and the actions of persons. Moore´s view is that the meaning of `right´ (and similarly, `good´ (See Chapter I of *Principia Ethica*) have an ascertainable meaning independent of assumptions made about the nature of the world and the actions of persons, and that seems incorrect.

Since ethical theories often attempt to define which among the alternative actions are right, at the foundations of these theories is the question, "What is the point of action?" The consequentialist reply is, "The whole point of action is to produce the desired effect." For example, last night I went to the store to buy groceries so that I could make dinner. I had two choices: either stay home or go to the store. Staying home has the effect of my going hungry. Going to the store (taken with some other actions) has the effect of my eating dinner. Now, isn´t the whole point of going to the store to avoid the effect of going hungry and to realize the effect of eating dinner? This example is typical of millions of actions people undertake on a daily basis. Therefore, if the analysis of action leads to the idea that actions are almost always undertaken in order to produce some desired effect then this leads to consequentialism, for it also directs our attention to the effects of actions.

If consequentialism is not true by definition then what reasons and arguments can be given in support of it? Joel J. Kupperman asks this question when he writes

RIGHT AND OUGHT

in "Vulgar Consequentialism":

> There are a number of things that ought to make us suspicious of... consequentialism...One is that if consequentialism is a highly general theory in ethics there ought to be arguments for it...Mill's Utilitarianism is a classic example of the missing argument, the philosophical dog that does not bark. (p. 323)

If consequentialism is not true by definition then it requires arguments to support it. There is a short passage in Utilitarianism in which Mill does sketch out an argument that, while not being a proof, does lend support to consequentialism. Mill's view seems to be that actions are essentially inseparable from their effects, for he writes in Chapter I (p. 2):

> All action is for the sake of some end, and rules of action, it seems natural to suppose, must take their whole character and color from the end to which they are subservient.

This argument is quite simple and straightforward. The reason why we act the way we do is to produce some desired effect (the "end"), and this suggests, though does not entail, that the ethical character of an action depends upon its effects. If so, we should examine the effects of actions and base our "rules of action" (our ethics) upon them. Mill's point is well-taken. The purpose of an action (or the reason why it is undertaken) is rarely for the sake of some abstract principle or intrinsic qualities of the action. We act to produce some desired effect, although we are often unsuccessful and something less than the desired effect is produced. If we are successful then it is reasonable to evaluate the action through an examination of its effects. If we are unsuccessful then the effects are still relevant, but the evaluation of the action is more complex, since we must now account for the intended effects of the action, the actual effects, and why the intended effects were not produced. Yet, the conclusion remains. Its effects is an important characteristic of an action, and therefore, ought to be included in its ethical evaluation.

RIGHT AND OUGHT

To further defend consequentialism, we may note that there is a clear and important distinction between performing an action and the motivation that precedes it. Again, this is also Mill's view, for he writes in <u>A System of Logic</u> (p. 42):

> Now what is an action? Not one thing, but a series of two things: the state of mind called volition, followed by an effect. The volition or intention to produce the effect is one thing; the effect produced in consequence of the intention, is another thing; the two together constitute the action.

This quote is somewhat confusing, since Mill is saying that an action is both the volition and the effect. At least, it is clear that he is committed to the distinction, and in the quotation taken from <u>Utilitarianism</u>, he claims that the rules of action are dependent upon their ends. Therefore, I think it is clear that Mill means to say that an analysis of action includes two separate factors, the motivation which precedes it and the effects which follow it, and that in the ethical evaluation of an action, we should separate the volition from the effects, and this is consistent with consequentialism.

Mill discusses his view that the motivation of the agent is a matter separate from the ethical evaluation of the agent's actions in a footnote to <u>Utilitarianism</u>. The topic is an example of a tyrant who saves a drowning man so that he might further torture him. The example is meant to show that we would hesitate to describe this as the right action, and yet, it has the effect of rescuing a drowning man, and so, presumably, the effects of the action are irrelevant. Mill observes correctly that the saving of a drowning man is only a partial account of the effects, and that when all is told, the effects are deleterious. The force of the counterexample rests on the evil motive of the tyrant. Mill's explanation both clarifies and introduces new complexities:

> The morality of the action depends entirely upon the intention--that is, upon what the agent <u>wills to do</u>. But

RIGHT AND OUGHT

> the motive, that is, the feeling which makes him will so to do, if it makes no difference in the act, makes none in the morality: though it makes a great difference in our moral estimation of the agent, especially if it indicates a good or bad habitual <u>disposition</u>--a bent of character from which useful, or from which hurtful actions are likely to arise. (p. 18)

First, Mill´s view as stated in this passage varies from the view I am defending. His view seems to be that the ethical evaluation of an action depends on what the agent "wills to do", as opposed to my view that only the action´s actual effects are relevant to its ethical evaluation. I agree with Mill that the agent´s psychological properties preceding the action are a separate issue that merits a separate, consequentialistically based evaluation. I include the purpose of the action within this class, if "purpose" refers to a psychological property of the agent. Mill is not clear on this point. If the "purpose" is identified with the intended effects of the action, and if the action is unsuccessful, then the purpose only exists as a psychological property of the agent. If so then the evaluation of the action falls back to the agent apart from the actual effects of the action, and we disagree. If the agent´s "purpose" is the effects of the action, and if the action is successful, then the purpose and the effects are identical, and we are in agreement.

The distinction between the effects of an action and the motivation that precedes it is well founded. An action is a concrete event, a motion that is impersonal as it becomes part of the causal nexus. Motivation is entirely personal to the agent. An action and its effects are open to observation, except when the effects reenter the private mental lives of persons. Thus, there are good reasons behind the distinction between motivation and action, and so, there are good reasons for keeping them distinct in ethics.

What I find especially admirable about consequentialists is that they accept full responsibility for the effects of their actions. To hold any other view allows the evasion of responsibility, because to withhold judgment when actions result in undesirable effects is to avoid culpability. It is self-deception to reason, "I have made myself virtuous", or "I haven´t violated anyone´s rights", or "I obeyed the law", and then to conclude, "And thus, I am a moral person, for I did the right thing.", when the actual effects of your actions are much less desirable than they could have been. If there is some way that we could alter the course of history to avoid some great disaster then if we failed to do so, non-consequentialists might be satisfied with the consolation, "Well, we were virtuous, we didn´t violate anyone´s rights, and we obeyed the law." I would not be so satisfied.

I suspect that the best arguments for consequentialism have their basis in the tie between taking responsibility for one´s action and one´s concept of personal identity. I find the effects of my actions closely tied to who I think I am, not that these effects are all that I wish they would be. We say, "If I only knew then what I know now!" Not taking responsibility for these consequences has the effect of deemphasizing the importance of my actions, which in turn, has the effect of a feeling of detachment from world events. Taking responsibility for the effects of my actions is a bridge between the ethics of the subjective process of deciding and willing to do an action and the objective effects of the action. Since taking responsibility is an intentional relation between these subjective and objective elements of an action, and if I am correct in assuming that there is no necessary connection between these two elements, then there is no deductive proof for the position. I take responsibility for the effects of my actions and, so, I am open to be praised or blamed for them.

It is a sign of maturity when a child begins to take responsibility for his or her actions. Saying, "I threw the rock, and I will pay to replace the broken window", amounts to the child´s taking responsibility for the effects of his or her actions, even if, at the crucial moment, he or she had not thought of the connection between throwing rocks and windows breaking. Likewise, adopting any view other than consequentialism is immature, if it amounts to evading the responsibility for the effects of one´s own actions, or in the case of a group action, avoiding responsibility for the effects of a cooperative action.(3)

AN ANALYSIS OF FREEDOM

The preceding view leads to the odd implication that the right action is not always the action that an individual (or group) ought to perform. Yet, I do hold that this is correct. I understand `ought´ to mean `be morally obligated´, and people can only be morally obligated to try their best at maximizing overall benefits. There are cases in which people try to produce the best possible effects, but fail because of unforseeable factors, and thus, they have done all that they ought to do, but have not done what is right. What is true is that we always ought to try to discover and perform the right action. We ought to perform the action (or actions) that we believe will probably produce the best consequences, but if we are mistaken then the action best determined to be the one we ought to perform will not be right.(4)

3. AN ANALYSIS OF FREEDOM

Consequentialism provides a method by which actions may be evaluated so that we can recognize and perform the action with maximum overall benefits. If consequentialism is a doctrine of practical significance then we must presuppose the power to make a chosen alternative happen. I am defending consequentialism on the basis of some common-sense assumptions, the complete defense of

---

3. I argue that consequentialists taking responsibility for their actions is a substitute for the usual view, that consequentialism is the only rational standard. I agree with Stubbs that there other rational standards than consequentialism. I hold that the "absolutism" she defends might be rational, but does not satisfactorily respond to the point about "responsibility". See "The Pros and Cons of Consequentialism", pp. 500-503.

4. The reasoning here is similar to that in Chapter VII of Foundations of Ethics by W.D. Ross. Therein, Ross concludes: "...we must maintain the complete non-dependence of moral goodness and rightness upon one another. For an action´s being morally good depends mainly on the motive from which it is done, and the goodness of the motive neither guarantees nor is guaranteed by the nature of the results that the act actually produces." (p. 165)

AN ANALYSIS OF FREEDOM

which is not within the scope of this essay. An assumption I will now examine in greater detail is that human beings usually have the freedom and power to choose an alternative action and make it happen.

If there is such a thing as human freedom then four conditions must be satisfied. FIRST, there must be several alternative actions available to us. SECOND, we must have sufficient knowledge of these alternatives. THIRD, we must be able to freely choose a desired outcome that matches one of these alternatives. And FOURTH, we must be able to make the chosen outcome happen.

Since there are cases in which several alternative actions exist for a person, we must adopt something other than a deterministic theory to account for these alternatives. Freedom requires more than alternative actions that are merely possible in some watered-down sense of possibility. It is not enough that it is only logically possible that I visit my mother this summer for it significantly to be an alternative action. Nor do I mean mere epistemic possibility, meaning that it is possible that I shall visit Mom, given the limits of my knowledge of the situation. It isn't just that I don't know if I'll be seeing Mom. The question is yet undecided. There is a problem with thinking, "Well, if I only knew how I will be choosing then I would know", for this is not a true case of epistemic possibility. From the fact that you are in a position to choose, it follows that the alternatives from which you are choosing are still open, and so, there is no possibility of knowing how you will choose prior to your making the choice. If it is possible to know how you would be choosing then you would not really be in the position of choice, since in the position of choice it is assumed that you might choose among several different alternatives open to you.

It would be inappropriate to delve too far into Possible Worlds theory in this essay. There are less controversial ways of speaking that I might employ, but I feel at ease with the language of Possible Worlds, and those who are not comfortable should still be able to appreciate the arguments to follow by abstracting from them any controversial metaphysical and epistemological ramifications they see as being implied by the theory. If we are to proceed, we need a consistent way

AN ANALYSIS OF FREEDOM

of framing a discussion of alternative courses of action, for as J.J.C. Smart writes in "An outline of a system of utilitarian ethics" (p. 8):

> The semantics for `would´ gets us into talk about possible worlds, which are dubious entities...consider a sentence like `If it rains Smith´s action is right.´ A non-cognitivist would perhaps interpret this as expressing approval of Smith´s action in a possible world in which it is raining. However ethics...probably needs the notion of a possible world, dubious or not, since it is concerned with alternative possible actions...

So, I will use the language of Possible Worlds without going very far into the metaphysical aspects of the theory, for, at least, it is one way of framing the discussion of human action and the alternative possible actions with which we are confronted.

I will point out one fault in Possible Worlds theory. It suggests that possible alternatives are discrete, when usually they are continuous. The theory suggests that separate possible alternatives exist in separate possible worlds, which seems mistaken, and is, I think, one of the major obstacles to overcome in adopting the theory. For instance, if I am in a field then there are an infinite number of bearings and courses that I may follow. These different bearings and courses are not really discretely placed in separate worlds, but instead constitute a very complex continuum of possible outcomes determined by the many paths that I may follow. So, often, possibilities are continuous, but the idea of there being different possible worlds suggests that possibilities are discretely placed in a context of separate possible worlds.

An election, especially one that does not allow write-in candidates, creates an artificial setting where there truly is an either/or situation. Either you vote for one of the candidates or you don´t vote at all. Unlike the example of choosing a bearing in an open field, the alternative actions in an election are discrete and thus, thinking of them as making up possible worlds is not misleading. Elections also

AN ANALYSIS OF FREEDOM

eliminate a complexity that enters into most other settings. Voting for Smith at 8 a.m. amounts to the same thing as voting for Smith at 8 p.m. The vote is counted, and so has the same impact no matter at what time it is made. This is not true in most cases. Driving to see Mom Sunday morning is very different from driving to see her Sunday afternoon.

There are, no doubt, some misleading ontological implications that arise from using the Possible Worlds model, but I can see none in using the Possible Worlds model in the context of decision theory as applied to ethics. Picturing alternatives as discrete choices framed in the Possible Worlds model gives us a useful way of comparing the alternatives available to us. Deliberation about alternatives is an important type of thinking that everyone regularly engages in, and as philosophers, we need to develop a method by which this thinking can be clearly understood. Possible Worlds theory applies nicely to the analysis of human actions because each alternative action exists in a complete situation, a world. The possibility of my visiting Mom cannot exist apart from the world as it will be while I am visiting Mom. If I stay home then there is the world existing as a complete situation that contains that alternative.

An account of freedom that employs the Possible Worlds model describes a setting in which possible alternative actions involve separate choices that result in separate Possible Worlds. In the election example, there is a Possible World in which I vote for Smith and a different Possible World in which I vote for Jones. These Possible Worlds, with the respective alternative actions that they contain are forever distinct, because if I vote for Smith then I will always be someone who voted for Smith, and similarly, if I vote for Jones. The Possible World in which the first choice is included will always be distinct from the other because any future alternatives within it will always be alternatives for "I who voted for Smith", and so this one choice will affect the relation I have to other subsequent choices and make them distinguishable from all the choices and events in the world as it would have been if I had voted for Jones.

As required by the second condition I stated as being necessary for human freedom, it is not enough

AN ANALYSIS OF FREEDOM

that alternatives exist for us to be free, we must also have some knowledge of them. If some action were available to the dinosaurs that would have led to their survival, it would have been of no help to them, because they lacked the intelligence necessary to be aware of such an alternative. Freedom requires that you choose an alternative action and make it happen. Without knowledge of the alternatives, you cannot make a choice, and thus, your freedom can be bound by your ignorance. How it is that we are able to make one alternative happen to the exclusion of the others is a difficult question that I am presently unable to fully explain. Action within Possible Worlds theory seems to be more a matter of destruction than creation, probably a metaphysically misleading implication of the theory. Visiting Mom destroys the alternative of staying home and converts the alternative of visiting Mom into the real event of visiting Mom. Once one alternative is realized, the other possible alternative actions cannot at that moment be realized, and so become impossible.

Consequentialism comes to bear at the third step, our being able to choose between alternative actions. Each alternative action will have its own unique set of effects. The action that has the best consequences is the right action and so, it is the action that we ought to try to discover and perform. For each alternative action, there is a possible world that corresponds to its effects placed in a complete situation. The identification of the right action resembles the Leibnizian concept of Best of all Possible Worlds in his "Monadology" (Paragraphs 53-55), although Leibniz´s theory presents a different picture of how and why one of many Possible Worlds becomes actual. In Leibniz´s view, God chooses and makes actual the best of all Possible Worlds. I am presenting a theory that the right action is the one that produces the maximum overall benefits, and is the one that results in the best of all Possible Worlds.

Performing the right action usually begins by choosing the right action. Consequentialism guides us in making that choice but it does not provide the ultimate criterion by which competing sets of consequences are to be rated. Consequentialism is not a normative theory that defines "the Good". It is a method of applying some preconceived concept of value to the ethical evaluation of actions. If happiness is

AN ANALYSIS OF FREEDOM

"the Good" then the right action is the one that results in the greatest happiness. If "the Good" is something other than happiness then consequentialism is adjusted accordingly.

Possible Worlds theory gives us a framework in which consequentialism can be clearly formulated because consequentialism applies to alternative actions and a Possible Worlds theory provides a clear picture of the relations between alternative actions. To illustrate this point, consider the following example: I have alternative actions "A" and "B" available to me. "A" is going to see Mom this weekend and "B" is staying home. Each of these alternative actions leads to two additional alternatives respectively, yielding four different overall courses of action, "AC", "AD", "BE", and "BF". "AC" is going to see Mom and taking her to the beach. "AD" is going to see Mom and staying at her house. "BE" is staying home and studying. "BF" is staying home and watching television. The value of these different consequences, assuming that each can be taken in themselves apart from alternatives to which they lead, are, let us suppose, rated so that "A" results in zero units of value, "B" results in ten units, "C" results in forty units, "D" results in zero units, "E" results in ten units, and "F" results in 20 units; all of which is represented by the following diagram: (5)

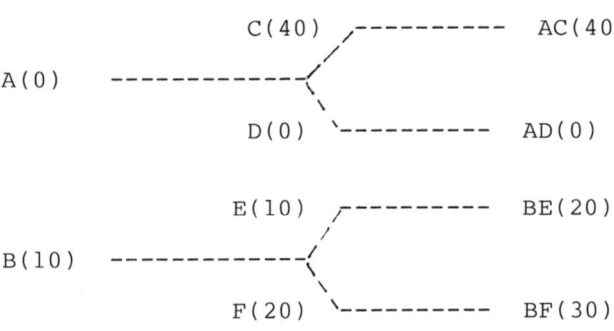

---
5. The diagram and analysis is similar to that given by Sobel in "Rule-utilitarianism", pp. 147-148.

AN ANALYSIS OF FREEDOM

I am also assuming that actions "C" and "D" are tied to action "A", and I also assume that actions "E" and "F" are tied to action "B", meaning, for instance, that action "F" is possible only if action "B" is first performed. Different actions lead to separate sets of alternative actions. "A" is going to see Mom and "B" is staying home. "AC" is going to see Mom and then taking her to the beach. The point is that action "B", staying home, leads to alternatives separate from action "A", for you cannot take Mom to the beach without first travelling to see her. So, "BC" does not designate a possible alternative action, although abstractly it is a course of action that would result in fifty points, a rating higher than any of the other alternatives. If consequentialism defines `right action´ as `action that produces the best consequences´, and if "A" and "B" are the only alternatives, then which of these two actions is right?

There really is no definitive answer to this question because the ordinary definition of consequentialism is ambiguous. Neither "A" nor "B" is right because there really is no simple quality equal to the consequences of either action, since the consequences vary according to other future actions and choices. I wouldn´t say that "B" is right because the average value of "BE" and "BF" is higher than the average value of "AC" and "AD". In this example, it is assumed that each of the alternatives are known and can be realized by choosing and acting on them. It seems that the only answer that is consistent with the aims of consequentialism is to say that it is only right to perform both actions "A" and "C".

Therefore, consequentialism cannot always provide an answer to the question of some particular action being right or wrong and instead, once all the options are made clear; it prescribes a series of actions that has the best overall consequences. As a decision procedure to be applied to particular situations, consequentialism is less than perfect, since we rarely know all of the effects of a particular action. Consequentialism provides an adequate decision procedure when applied to a complete series of actions. It counsels us to perform the series of actions that have the best overall consequences. This ambiguity in consequentialism has been the source of a great amount of confusion. I will show that many of the objections

AN ANALYSIS OF FREEDOM

raised against consequentialism are unfounded, once this ambiguity is made apparent.

The next example I wish to present involves another level of generality. In the preceding example, it was assumed that an individual was making a choice in isolation from the choices of others. There is another added complication to consequentialism when the actions of several persons become entwined, as is usually the case. Consider this situation: Smith and Jones live with Brutus on a desert island. Brutus is the strongest of the three and acts like a tyrant, which makes the lives of Smith and Jones miserable. Four alternative courses of action become available to Smith and Jones at some key moment:

1 & 2. Either Smith or Jones, but not both, challenge Brutus, which results in defeat and even worse conditions on the island, or

3. they will do nothing and conditions will remain the same, or

4. they will both rebel, defeat Brutus, and improve the overall conditions on the island.

The right action is the one that results in the best of all Possible Worlds which is #4, the Possible World resulting from the rebellion of both Smith and Jones. For reasons similar to those given in the discussion of the last example, I claim that as a decision procedure, Consequentialism cannot provide a definitive answer to the question, "Should Smith rebel?". The outcome of Smith's rebellion depends on Jones' decision, so there is no single thing equal to the effect of Smith's action.(6) Instead, consequentialism can only answer the question, what should they both do?, and in the above situation (things are rarely this simple), the answer is, they should cooperate and both rebel!

----

6. For a more detailed analysis that draws similar conclusions without using Possible Worlds theory, see Donald Regan's analysis of the "snowball argument" in <u>Utilitarianism and Cooperation</u>, pp. 43-53.

4. GENERAL CONSEQUENTIALISM

The general aim of utilitarianism is to maximize overall benefits for the community. The preceding section shows that when consequentialism is applied to isolated examples from a narrow perspective, it does not provide a decision procedure that leads to the maximization of overall benefits. Consequentialism is consistent with the general aim of utilitarianism only when it is applied at the most general level, for if we take the principles suggested by the two preceding examples to their logical end, it follows that a consequentialistic decision theory that fulfills the aims of utilitarianism must be based on a complete series of actions of everyone taken over an extended length of time.

As a methodology to be applied to ethical issues, the efficacy of Consequentialism is limited by our ability to isolate and compare the anticipated effects of our actions. The preceding examples show that decisions made over a series of alternatives are more reliable than decisions made separately at each junction, and that only through cooperation on the part of those people whose actions and their effects are entwined can the combined effects of their actions be maximized. Since the decision theory must be based on the broadest possible base to satisfy aims of utilitarianism, it is reasonable to put the theory of moral obligation on the same basis. What follows from this assumption is that, under General Consequentialism (7) (as I shall call it), ethical obligation is primarily defined as an obligation of a large group over a whole range of actions. If the overall aim is to maximize benefits then the particular obligations of individuals must fall under and be determined by the more general theory of obligation.

----

7. David O. Brink argues that "there is no successful moral objection to utilitarianism from the personal point of view", for reasons similar to those I am working towards. He says, "there is good reason to think...that agents should adopt a differential concern for their own projects and the welfare of others close to them." See "Utilitarianism and the Personal Point of View", pp. 417-427.

GENERAL CONSEQUENTIALISM

In support of the preceding view, observe that there does not actually exist the "effect" that can be attributed to any single action, except in the rare case (if there be any) in which the action does not lead to future alternatives. If a person commits suicide then this peculiar type of action does have an "effect" that precludes any future choices and alternatives on the part of that person, although, of course, the act of suicide will affect the lives of others. From every other action there follows a future filled with choices and alternatives. Choosing to act in some particular way only limits future choices and alternatives. Excepting suicide, the "effect" of an action is a very complex set of possibilities, none of which is actual. Only one of these possible outcomes will become actual. The actual outcome is a product of several choices and actions. Since I am defining `right´ in terms of the actual outcome that is most beneficial then `right´ can only pertain to a series of actions that have as their result the actual effects that are most beneficial.

A similar argument supports the thesis that `right´ fundamentally applies to the actions of everyone taken together. The actions of a single person have no separate "effect" in a world in which the impact of each person´s actions is entwined with the actions of others. The only exception is the case of a person who is truly isolated and incapable of rejoining society. There is no single actual effect of an individual´s action, instead, there is a complex set of possibilities that involve the actions and decisions of others. If `right´ means actually productive of maximum benefits then the actions of individuals are neither right nor wrong in isolation from the actions of others. Thus, `right´ fundamentally pertains to a series of actions as undertaken by everyone, and a particular action by an individual is `right´ only if it coincides with this more general course of action. According to General Consequentialism, a particular action is defined as being right in virtue of its being a part of an overall course of action that maximizes benefits. Since it has been shown that benefits cannot be maximized from the perspective of isolated actions, the fallacy of composition is committed by reasoning that the sum of isolated actions that aim towards maximum benefits will be equivalent to the benefits of cooperative actions based upon a wider perspective. The property of being productive of maximum benefits cannot be properly attributed to isolated actions. An isolated action rarely has an identifiable effect, no less the identifiable effect of maximizing benefits. Since the determination of the consequences of an isolated action depends on future choices that are made independently of the action, several different sets of effects follow (or more precisely, are made possible) from the action. The effects cannot be calculated until these future choices have been made, so it is quite possible that a single isolated action leads to several sets of effects with very different consequences. A single isolated action might lead both to creation of utopia and the destruction of the universe, depending upon future choices and actions. I cannot say that the isolated action is right or wrong, only that within its effects are possible outcomes such that if they became actual then they would be right or wrong.

There are problems with the theory. I am developing General Consequentialism so that it is consistent with the utilitarian ideal of achieving the maximum benefits. A world in which maximum possible benefits are achieved is a utopian ideal. Thus, General Consequentialism is a theory based upon an abstract world model that has only a theoretical basis. Since the ideal is practically unattainable, the theory only provides a theoretical model that requires interpretation when and if it is applied to actual cases. The biggest problem for General Consequentialism (and most other utilitarian theories) is its tendency to demand that individuals subjugate their personal life projects to the grand plans proposed by the theory. (I further address these problems in Chapters Three and Four.) The society proposed by the fully developed version of Qualitative Utilitarianism is one that provides for an environment that stimulates personal creativity and experimentation within boundaries established to protect the individual and the public. The thesis is a paternalistic view that recognizes and promotes "tried-and-true" lifestyles that secure both the happiness of individuals and the welfare of the community.

General Consequentialism asks us to consider the results of a long series of choices and actions, but in practice we must make each choice individually at its proper moment. The idea of choosing a course of action over my lifetime based on my prediction of its overall outcome is too complex an idea to seriously entertain. I say that the alternative actions of everyone taken together must be evaluated in terms of benefits, and yet, this is a task of such high complexity that no computer we have today is able to undertake it. Taken to the extreme, the theory is that only the effects of the actions of everyone taken together over the past, present, and future of the universe are actual in the sense that the effects of a particular action are never completely tallied, as their effects and after-effects continue on and on.

The defense of General Consequentialism against these kinds of objections begins with the observation of the actual complexity of the human situation. The theory is complex because the human situation is complex. Every attempt at simplification lays the theory open to counter-examples and <u>reductio</u> arguments. To simplify by limiting the effects of an action to those that occur within 20 years lays the theory open to counterexamples that are based on effects of actions beyond that limit. If the effects of some action were to produce utopia for 20 years, say by the reckless consumption of our natural resources or by producing mountains of nuclear waste, and follow with centuries of misery, then the action clearly is not right. To exclude the effects of any one person from our calculations lays the theory open to a <u>reductio</u> argument based on the idea that the effects (taken abstractly) of everyone else´s actions taken together are desirable, but the effects with the extra person added become catastrophic.

When the theory is judiciously applied to practical life, it makes perfectly good sense. On the assumption that the course of action to be undertaken is the one that results in maximum benefits, General Consequentialism recommends that individuals cooperate in establishing long-term programs aimed at the welfare of the public. This coincides with the common sense idea that a lifetime of disjointed decisions based on the particular situation at hand tends to be narrow-sighted and counterproductive. General Consequentialism also emphasizes cooperation instead of each individual trying to solve problems in his or her own way, which also coincides with common sense. General Consequentialism is an improvement over consequentialism as ordinarily understood. To prove this point, I shall examine some typical objections to consequentialism in the light of the improved theory, and show that the application of General Consequentialism diminishes the power of these objections.

Consider the Voter's Paradox (8). In a presidential election, a consequentialist analysis of a particular decision by an isolated individual would likely yield that it is better to stay home than to bother voting. The chances of one vote changing the results of the election are small, but the chances of enjoying staying home more than waiting in line at the polls are very good. This seems absurd to most people, and so seems to render the theory implausible. Some people would claim that it is our duty to vote, regardless of the consequences. The application of General Consequentialism yields a different conclusion. There is a general obligation to produce the best overall consequences, and that requires responsible and capable leadership. So, there is a general obligation for voters to cooperate in order to elect responsible and capable leaders, and thus, the individual is obligated (within reason) to participate in this process.

Littering is another example. If I am backpacking in the wilderness and have carried a Coke bottle several miles from the nearest trash barrel then what should I do when the bottle is emptied? Should I carry the bottle out of the wilderness or should I toss it in the brushy canyon below? The benefits of tossing the bottle are that I will be saved the trouble of packing the bottle out of the wilderness. It is highly unlikely that packing the bottle out will be of any benefit to me. When backpacking, every ounce counts. There is the slim chance that the bottle will come in handy as a canteen or for some other purpose along the way. The major liability of tossing the bottle is that it might reenter into the lives of other people in a deleterious manner. There is the small chance that someone will someday come by the bottle and be offended by seeing the bottle as trash. It ruins a wilderness experience to come by trash, but the chance of this happening is small, since the bottle was thrown in a brushy,

---

8. This example is discussed in <u>The Theory of Morality</u>, p. 195.

untraveled canyon. According to consequentialism (as often understood), it is probably right to toss the bottle. When General Consequentialism is applied to the problem, we arrive at a different solution. The community is obligated to handle its garbage in a way that preserves the beauty of the environment, which is the principle that consequentialism seems to violate in the littering example taken from a limited perspective. So, to some degree, I am obligated to carry out the bottle, as this obligation falls under the greater obligation of the community, but there is no clear answer to the particular question at hand. This is an improvement over the usual consequentialist solution, and is, I think, an honest and reasonable appraisal of the situation.

I shall next compare General Consequentialism to "Utilitarianian Generalization", as stated by David Lyons in <u>Forms</u> <u>and</u> <u>Limits</u> <u>of</u> <u>Utilitarianism</u> (p. 3) He writes:

> ...<u>general</u> utilitarian considerations concern the total effects that <u>could</u> be produced if all acts similar to the one in question, which could be performed, actually were performed.

Utilitarian Generalization is so named because of its similarity to logical generalization. It evaluates a particular action `some x did y in situation z´ by reference to the effects of the generalization `what if all x´s did y-like in z-like situations?´. This sort of counterfactual is entirely different than the theoretical basis of General Consequentialism. Utilitarian Generalization begins with the particular action, generalizes to the abstract `what if everyone acted similarly in similar situations?´, and then returns to evaluate the particular action through an examination of the generalization. General Consequentialism begins at the level of the actual effects of everyone´s actions taken together over a long period of time and then evaluates particular actions in reference to the more general perspective.

The analysis given by the application of Utilitarian Generalization to the Voter´s Paradox and Littering in the Wilderness example is much less plausible than that given by General Consequentialism. Utilitarian

GENERAL CONSEQUENTIALISM

Generalization asks us to consider, `What if everyone failed to vote and failed to properly dispose of their litter when it became inconvenient?´. The answer is that the effects would be deleterious, and thus, the individual has a reason to vote and a reason to dispose of their litter properly. According to General Consequentialism, the evaluation of a particular action cannot be made apart from the relation of it to the actions of everyone else taken over a long period of time. If you are cooperating with a group, and if without you, they have enough votes to win the election for the best candidate, then you no longer have any good reason to vote, and should be out performing some other function necessary to achieving maximum overall benefits. If James Bond, as an agent of the British government, is on a mission to destroy a mad scientist´s secret laboratory, which poses a threat to all civilization, then he has no reason at all to return to England to vote in the upcoming election or to worry about the litter that results from the destruction of the laboratory. His role in the production of maximum benefits is different from the role of every other citizen, and so `What ought he to do?´ is a question separate from the abstract consideration, `what if everyone acted that way?´. The two theories coincide only in cases in which everyone has approximately the same function in producing maximum overall benefits. The voting and littering examples are especially suited to Utilitarian Generalization because, usually, we all approximately have the same role in that regard. In most cases, we do not share a common role and so, it makes little sense to ask `What if everyone acted this way?´.

Finally, consequentialism is seen by some to be a license to perform horrible acts in the name of the greater good. It is difficult to assign a degree of horribleness to an action, since an action´s being horrible depends upon its offensiveness, and this varies from person to person. Alan Donagan finds that, in some cases, consequentialism condones cannibalism and killing innocent people. (9) Since the performance of any kind of action might be necessary in order to

---

9. *The Theory of Morality*, pp. 172-189. Also see *Forms and Limits of Utilitarianism*, pp. 12-24.

maximize overall benefits, then it does follow that, according to consequentialism, there is no specific kind of action that is forbidden. If we are appalled by a particular kind of action, then this is in itself a noteworthy consequence of that kind of action, and thus, constitutes consequentialist grounds for its being forbidden.

What is misleading about these examples is that when we focus on a hypothetical case, even if it is given as being a once-in-a-lifetime situation, it is difficult not to slip into a generalization when giving our response to the ethics of the situation. It might seem that we are condoning a horrible kind of action by holding that it is justified in a particular case. Consequentialists despise cannibalism and torturing innocent people as much as anyone on account of the generally undesirable effects of these actions. Yet, if killing and eating an innocent boy, who is near death anyway, is the only means for two shipwrecked sailors to survive then I do not find it to be so horrible that they do so. The sailors are faced with two horrible alternatives, starvation or cannibalism. Donagan doesn't seem to find the horrors of starvation to be nearly as horrible as cannibalism. A consequentialist makes little of the distinction between death caused by pneumonia and death caused by cannibalism. Both are equally horrible because both equally have the effect of no longer being able to enjoy life. Assenting to a particular case does not imply condoning cannibalism in general. It is not recommending that we regularly eat one another whenever it is convenient. A consequentialist examines the situation and all of the alternatives, and then makes his choice on an entirely humanistic basis. When properly understood, consequentialism is not such a horrible theory at all.

5. THE PARADOX OF CONSEQUENTIALISM

The Paradox of Consequentialism is that, even if the theory be granted, to hold it and actually put it into practice might actually produce effects that are less than the best possible. In other words, the paradox is based on the idea that it is likely that the adoption of some theory other than consequentialism leads to the best consequences. So, it seems, a consequentialist should hold an ethical theory different from consequentialism. If this is correct then the

THE PARADOX OF CONSEQUENTIALISM

legitimacy of consequentialism is called into question, for if the adoption of a theory leads to effects opposite to those valued by it then the theory is only of speculative interest.(10)

It is correct that, taken from the limited perspective of individuals deciding on isolated actions, adopting consequentialism leads to problems. A promise made by a consequentialist would have little meaning, because it is likely that he would find another option that leads to more overall benefits than fulfilling the promise. If a consequentialist takes out a student loan then it is unlikely that repaying the loan will be more beneficial than donating the money to charity. The negative effect of losing his good credit rating and the financial loss of $5,000 on the part of the bank doesn´t compare to the benefits of buying fifty tons of rice to feed starving children.

What appears to be a problem for consequentialism is, again, really a problem that originates in decision theory. General Consequentialism clarifies consequentialism as a decision theory so that when it is applied to standard problems they appear in a much different light. If everyone held General Consequentialism and if it were applied to the series of actions that maximized benefits, then there would not exist nearly as many complications to meeting one´s promises. Also, in the concrete case, if there really is no other way to achieve significantly superior benefits then the consequentialist is properly bound to break his promise. If, all things considered, there is no other way to feed the children then he should break his promise and donate the money to charity. What is repugnant about these counterexamples is that we know that if everyone broke promises in every instance that they discovered some marginally beneficial alternative then there would arise the negative consequence of living in a society in which the promises of our fellow citizens are unreliable. But, if it really were true that in the context of creating a future of maximum benefits that a promise needed to be broken then it ought to be broken.

----

10. Kupperman suggests, and then dismisses, the alternative of a consequentialist keeping his view a secret in "Vulgar Consequentialism", p. 322.

ACT AND RULE CONSEQUENTIALISM

Thus, in the larger perspective, holding consequentialism is not counterproductive to its stated ends. Further, General Consequentialism provides a broader basis for the obligations of keeping promises, etc., than that of consequentialism as ordinarily understood. Since General Consequentialism provides a sound basis for the decision process by avoiding the ambiguities and pitfalls of plain consequentialism, it will tend to provide for maximum benefits, and thus, the paradox is broken.

Without supernatural interference or the "invisible hand" of Adam Smith, it is obvious that adopting General Consequentialism will result in consequences superior to those of any other theory. To think otherwise amounts to holding that we are on a "ship of fools", so incompetent that we are unable to plan for the future and realize our goals. Alan Donagan, in The Theory of Morality (p. 202) claims that adherence to the "common morality", which he believes to be non-consequentialistic, will never lead to "calamitous" consequences, and that we cannot know that the consequences of adopting any other theory than his will result in superior consequences. There is no way that I can prove my point beyond a doubt. What would happen as a result of a society adopting a moral code is an immensely complex question. I generalize from the idea that if a person desires to be surrounded by death, then he should try his best at being a murderer to the idea that if a society desires the best overall consequences then its citizens must consciously attempt to reach that goal. Mozart did not become a great musician by playing in his sandbox.

6. ACT AND RULE CONSEQUENTIALISM

In keeping with the identification of utilitarianism with consequentialism discussed in the Introduction, what I would be inclined to call `Act Consequentialism´ and `Rule Consequentialism´ are often now called `act-utilitarianism´ and `rule-utilitarianism´. The controversy between these two versions of consequentialism is itself a proper subject for a book-length essay. It involves important issues in generalization in ethics, action theory, decision theory, and the place of rules in an ethical theory. General Consequentialism is a version of act-utilitarianism that stands clear of the standard objections to act-utilitarianism that form the impetus for the development of rule-utilitarianism. Thus, the act-utilitarianism/rule-utilitarianism controversy depends upon a mistaken assumption that is avoided by General Consequentialism.

Before we proceed, let's examine the definitions put forth by David Lyons in *Forms and Limits of Utilitarianism* (pp. 9-11):

> Act-utilitarianism is the theory that one should always perform acts the effects of which would be at least as good as those of any alternative.
>
> By rule-utilitarianism I shall mean that kind of theory according to which the rightness or wrongness of particular acts can (or must) be determined by reference to a set of rules having some utilitarian defence, justification, or derivation.

These definitions are somewhat misleading in that they suggest that the difference between act-utilitarianism and rule-utilitarianism is acting on a set of rules in the case of the latter and not acting on a set of rules in the case of the former. Rather, act-utilitarianism is consequentialism with a single rule: of all alternative courses of action, perform the one that is expected to provide the maximum overall benefits. Rule-utilitarianism is a form of consequentialism with rules that are to be followed, even if there is conflict with the single rule of act-utilitarianism. Otherwise, if the two theories always prescribe exactly the same actions then the distinction is of no practical importance.

Act-utilitarians and rule-utilitarians both aspire to the same goal: to maximize overall benefits for the community. No rule-utilitarian should ever ask us to act in a particular way simply to uphold some moral principle. That would violate the fundamental idea behind utilitarianism, that moral obligation is to be grounded in actual benefits for persons. The difference between rule-utilitarianism and act-utilitarianism is a matter of a conceptual difference and the differences in practical implications between the set of rules of the former and the single rule of the latter. The point is that there is a wide range in rule-utilitarianisms, some being not very different from act-utilitarianism to the opposite extreme of having consequences that are very different from those of act-utilitarianism. A problem for act-utilitarians is that without a set of simple-to-follow guidelines, such as those supplied by rule-utilitarianism, it is impossible to calculate the expected benefits of each alternative action available to us. In this respect, rule-utilitarians have the better theory. Act-utilitarians could still hold their ethical theory, but admit that, on practical grounds, it is often better to act on a set of rules, but this does not commit them to rule-utilitarianism on a theoretical level.

Rule-utilitarianism arose as a proposed solution to problems in the area of generalization in ethics. Lyons gives an example of one person picking a single orange from an orchard along a California freeway (pp. 2-3) This act, taken in itself, is insignificant in the harm done to the farmer, but what if each of the millions of Californians regularly did the same? Then, the farmer would be in big trouble. Of course, when the individual decides that one time to stop and pick an orange he or she is not choosing that everyone do likewise. There is, perhaps, a discrepency in wanting to pick the orange while not wanting to live in a world full of orange-snatchers. Rule-utilitarianism is an attempt to accomodate ethical generalization, for if a greater benefit accrues from ruling out such cases of stealing fruit, then a rule against stealing fruit is justified. The crucial difference between act-utilitarianism and rule-utilitarianism is that there are cases in which the act-utilitarian finds the rule-utilitarian to be inconsistent. As in the orange picking example, in the particular case there are more benefits expected from picking the orange than from following the rule that if generally adopted would maximize benefits. According to act-utilitarianism, you ought to pick the orange but according to rule-utilitarianism you should not. An act-utilitarian can even admit that it is a commendable rule, but in this case he still believes he should pick the orange, because that alternative has the most beneficial effects. Rule utilitarians reply, "I understand, but I am still not picking the orange". This seems inconsistent to the act-utilitarian, because the decision is based upon an isolated instance, and, in this case, picking the orange maximizes benefits. To do otherwise seems to run contrary to the aims of utilitarianism.(11)

It is at this point that I am holding that both the act-utilitarians and rule-utilitarians share a common, but mistaken, assumption. It is not surprising that it is assumed that an ethical theory should provide the correct answer when applied to individual cases, as is often true of scientific theories. For example, the general statement that bodies attract each other in proportion to the inverse square of the measurement of the distance between them applies to the force of gravity in the particular case of the Earth and its moon. The same applies to logic. The general law <u>modus ponens</u> applies to every case of reasoning in which a conditional statement and its antecedent are affirmed. Because of the peculiar nature of human choice, the usual general to particular relation does not hold in this area. As has been shown in the reasoning that leads to General Consequentialism, if we desire to maximize benefits, there is no way to devise a decision procedure that works in all individual cases taken in isolation. The only way to maximize benefits is to devise a mutual, long range strategy that applies to all of our decisions.

Rule-utilitarians want to both maximize consequences and have a general theory that applies to particular cases. I have shown that this is not always possible. My position is that there is no satisfactory solution to problems like the orange picking example, and that instead, consequentialism can only be consistently applied to the problem in which we are ultimately most interested, that being the complex situation in which all alternatives and all of their effects are laid open to us. At this point, the community can jointly choose the actions that, in fact, maximize overall benefits. This is not to deny that consequentialism often does

---

11. Stubbs makes the same point when she writes: "Given that the rule utilitarian wants to give his rules a consequentialistic justification, it is not difficult to convict him of irrationality when he refuses to break them on consequentialistic grounds". ("The Pros and Cons of Consequentialism", p. 501.)

work well when applied to isolated and hypothetical situations, for it does. I am holding that when all is made clear, many of the counter-examples presented against consequentialism, as ordinarily defined, are resolved by General Consequentialism.

7. A FINAL REJOINDER

As explained in the discussion of the Paradox of Consequentialism, I assume that the adoption of General Consequentialism will result in maximum overall benefits. Given any other theory, there must be a gap between the actual benefits of adopting that theory and adopting consequentialism. This gap, I assume, will be very real and very significant. Achieving less than the maximum overall benefits translates into human life as lowering the quality of life for real people, a very serious matter. And yet, this gap must be justified by any opposing theory. If non-consequentialists were facing the people who would be harmed by adoption of their theory, would they be able to explain why it is that they should suffer? If a consequentialist were placed in a similar situation, at least he could point to someone who benefits as a result of another's suffering. I am defending consequentialism because this gap ultimately defeats any other theory.

CHAPTER TWO

HEDONISM

1. HEDONISM AND HUMANISM

To a large degree, I find hedonism, the theory that only pleasure has intrinsic value, is often confused with humanism, the theory that all value is based on value for humans. At its best, humanism is not a crude favoritism for one´s own species. Humanism is not merely the theory that all ethical value is invested in the biological species Homo sapiens, and that, coincidentally, we are the only members of that species. It is not a queer kind of vanity that could be as well founded from the perspective of any other species. Rather, in its best formulations, humanism is based upon an analysis of the kind of entities we are. Humanists find that we are highly intelligent beings with the capacity of acting on rational principles, and so, it is justified that we are the basis of ethical value. Perhaps, we are the only beings that satisfy these criteria, but if some other highly intelligent beings of a different species were to appear then they might well be included within the "human" community. Thus, the name `humanism´ is misleading, since it suggests an unfounded favoritism towards a single biological species, when its real concern is human-like beings.

Also, the context of a treatise on ethics is that of one human writing for other humans with the subject generally being that of how our actions affect one another. In this context, one might hold that what is good for the individual is generally those things that are pleasures for that individual. If so, and if we assume the democratic ideal that the happiness of one human is equal in value to that of every other human, then this leads to the view that the right action is the one that maximizes overall pleasure for humans. In other words, I think that ethical hedonism often arises in a context in which it has already been assumed or proven that value is primarily value for humans. If hedonists were unaware of this human context then they might easily be perplexed as to the question of the intrinsic value of pleasure, if it was not pleasure for some entity like ourselves. I shall be speaking of hedonism based on humanism, not humanism based on hedonism.

HEDONISM AND HUMANISM

In the essay that follows, I shall disregard the question of animal pleasures, and only speak of pleasures for humans. That animals experience pleasure is a significant issue within hedonism, but is not important in regard to issues surrounding qualitative hedonism, the topic I am working towards. Humanistic hedonism leads to the view that there is nothing intrinsically valuable about the existence of pleasure apart from the fact that humans value it. Without a humanistic basis, a hedonist is led to hold that pleasure itself has intrinsic value, which leads to the vexing position that animal pleasures are of nearly the same value as human pleasures. If pleasure could exist apart from being pleasure for someone or something then I doubt if a hedonist would want to place value on such pleasure. Pleasure, taken in itself, as a monadic property, lacks intrinsic value. Only when something finds satisfaction in it, can pleasure be reasonably held as having value. From this it follows that an analysis of the value of pleasure should attend to the nature of pleasure as it exists in various relations to the people that it affects. Any interpretation of hedonism that does not carefully account for this conceptual link between hedonism and humanism (what I shall call simple hedonism) lies open to this kind of criticism.

Hedonistic Utilitarianism is the theory that the right action is the one that maximizes pleasure. In accordance with the thesis of the preceding chapter, I hold that an action is right if and only if it is part of that series of actions that has the greatest overall pleasure as its result. Simple hedonism takes pleasure as being a property that is intrinsically valuable in itself, even if it were not a part of human experience. This leads to the absurd position that if pleasure existed apart from personal experience then such pleasure also ought to be taken into account in the ethical evaluation of the effects of our actions.(12)

----

12. G.E. Moore´s interpretation of hedonism in Chapter III of <u>Principia Ethica</u> is an example of simple hedonism. Note that only simple hedonism commits the naturalistic fallacy, since it is the interpretation that <u>identifies</u> pleasure as being a simple property identical to "the Good".

HEDONISM AND HUMANISM

Simple hedonism is open to serious objections, as the case in which utilitarianism is said not allow for individual merit in the distibution of goods within the community, From simple hedonism it follows that there is no ethically relevant difference between punishing innocent people and punishing criminals, if both actions result in the same amount of pleasure, which does seem absurd.(13). Simple hedonism cannot account for the difference in different distributions of goods that have the same amount of pleasure, when these different distributions can be and often are ethically different. Under simple hedonism, if the net amount of pleasure and pain is the same in both distributions then one that is apparently unjust is no better than the other. Merely being aware of the humanistic basis of hedonism does not solve these problems for utilitarians, but it is an important consideration. Under the humanistic version of hedonism, two distributions with an equal amount of pleasure may differ ethically, if they are pleasures for different persons. Thus, at least, a distinction between an apparently just and an apparently unjust distribution can be made.

Within humanistic hedonism, there are two main links between humanism and hedonism. FIRST, the existence of pleasure is limited to particular episodes of human experience. SECOND, the value of pleasure depends on the fact that humans desire it. Simple hedonism is a theory based upon a mistaken idea of the nature of pleasure, and it leads to absurd consequences when incorporated in utilitarian theory. Utilitarianism based on simple hedonism calls for the maximization of pleasure. Utilitarianism based upon humanistic hedonism calls for maximizing human benefits, which is production of pleasure for humans in a way that most benefits them. The theories might seem identical, but their implications are quite different, as will be shown in the following chapter.

The main argument for hedonism is a simple one, and is based on humanistic grounds. In reply to any claim that we ought to act in a particular manner, it

---

13. The point is made in several articles, for example, McCloskey´s "A Non-Utilitarian Approach to Punishment", pp. 241-242.

is fair to ask, `What good is it to anyone?´ If an action cannot be shown to benefit someone then there seems to be no rational grounds for demanding that it be performed. Hedonists recognize that people generally desire pleasure. It seems clear that, once our basic needs are taken care of, there is nothing that is good for persons except pleasure. This becomes a more defensible position once the higher pleasures claimed by Qualitative Hedonism have been identified. Twice a day, Moslems lay out their rugs and pray to Allah. If Allah does not exist and if repeating the same prayers day after day is of little use to the Moslems then, according to humanistic hedonism, there is no reason that they ought to pray, for it is not doing anyone any good. The same applies to every other proposed obligation. If no one benefits, then why do it?

Hedonism is a theory that identifies pleasure as "the Good". Humanism is the view that "the Good" is primarily "the Good" in relation to humans. For practical purposes, from the point of view of Qualitative Utilitarianism, pleasure only exists as a part of human experience and is valued only because humans find it desirable. Without humanism, there is no philosophical support for hedonism. Therefore, there is an important connection between the two theories to which we must attend if we are to give a reasonable account of hedonism.

2. PSYCHOLOGICAL HEDONISM

Psychological Hedonism is the view that all voluntary actions are undertaken by individuals because they expect to gain pleasure or avoid pain as a result of the action, or conversely, if an individual has no expectation of gaining pleasure or avoiding pain as a result of the action then the individual lacks a motive to act in that way. Voluntary actions require that the source or impetus of the action fall within the powers of the agent. (See Aristotle´s <u>Nichomachean Ethics</u>, Book III.) The motivation of the agent may be called upon to explain why one particular action was undertaken instead of another. Yesterday, I went to the store because I was motivated to buy groceries so that I would avoid the pain of going hungry. That I desired to avoid pain, to some extent, explains why I went to the store. If the source of an action is outside of the agent's powers, like Dorothy being carried away by a tornado, or if the action happens by accident, then the action is involuntary. A motive is a reason in the sense that reference to it can explain an action. Thus, in respect to voluntary actions, once they have been chosen, the Principle of Sufficient Reason holds true. For each voluntary action, there is an explanation of why one alternative action was undertaken to the exclusion of the others.

A Psychological Hedonist holds that the agent's desire for pleasure and aversion to pain is sufficient to explain all of his voluntary actions. Thus, for every voluntary action, there is a reason that we may uncover such that it can be understood why that action and not some other alternative action was undertaken. For example, I am acting by writing an essay on hedonism. Insofar as it is a voluntary action, there must be reasons (broadly taken) that explain why I am writing this essay instead of performing one of the other alternative actions that I might have undertaken. There also must be reasons why I am writing this essay and not some other, and there must be reasons why I am writing this essay with these phrases and not some others.

In its weakest form, Psychological Hedonism is the view that every voluntary action is undertaken at least in part for the reason that pleasure (or avoiding pain) is expected to result from the action.(14) It follows that no voluntary action is undertaken without, at least, expecting some pleasure (or avoiding some pain). On this view, any action for which no pleasure can be expected is impossible or, in other words, expected pleasure (or avoiding pain) is a necessary condition for all voluntary actions.

In its strongest form, Psychological Hedonism is the view that every voluntary action is undertaken solely for the reason of expected pleasure (or avoiding

----

14. This weak form of Psychological Hedonism resembles Gosling's definition of hedonism as "if the action is chosen, then the final reason will have some reference to pleasure in it" in *Pleasure and Desire*, p. 9.

pain), from which it follows that expected pleasure is the only reason behind all voluntary acts, and from this it follows that nothing else but the expectation of pleasure (or avoiding pain) can be a reason behind a voluntary action. If I were to enumerate all possible actions that might be undertaken by any given individual then, according to Psychological Hedonism, the key to explaining why those actions were undertaken and not some others lies in understanding the agent's desire for pleasure. According to Strong Psychological Hedonism, the reason why some actions are undertaken and others not can always be explained by reference to the pleasure expected to result from those actions actually undertaken. If pleasure is the only motivation behind voluntary actions then the expectation of a greater pleasure is always more of a motivating factor than the expectation of a lesser pleasure. According to this theory, if I have more motivation to act in one way rather than another then I must act in that way. Thus, according to Strong Psychological Hedonism, I will always act in the way that I expect to result in the most pleasure. Strong Psychological Hedonism is incompatible with any account of human freedom, except the freedom to pursue only pleasure. There are actions ranging from those we expect to produce no pleasure to those we expect to produce a great deal of pleasure. Strong Psychological Hedonists hold that the alternative expected to produce the greatest amount of pleasure (with allowances made for pain) is the action that people will be most inclined to perform.

What follows in the next few paragraphs is a sketch of a theory of motivation much like the Psychological Hedonism put forth by John Stuart Mill in Utilitarianism (15). It is a theory based upon Psychological Determinism, the theory that one's present psychological state is entirely a product of one's past experiences, and the Principle of Association, the view that the mind links ideas presented to it as being together in space and time, even when there is no logical connection between them. From this theory it

----

15. See Chapters II. and IV. of Utilitarianism. For a further explanation of the Principle of Association, see Berger's Happiness, Justice, and Freedom, pp. 10-16.

follows that if "x" can be experienced by a person in association with something that is already desired by the person then "x" can become desired by that person. Since I will later be examining the Desire Theory of pleasure, this is relevant to hedonism. The theory that follows is not the view that I will be ultimately defending. For now, I only wish to show how theorists like Mill argue for Ethical Hedonism through appeals based on Psychological Hedonism.

We are born desiring pleasure and desiring to avoid pain (or detesting pain), although these desires are less sophisticated and complex than those of an adult. Generally, an infant desires to remain comfortable and desires to avoid feeling uncomfortable. One might say that an infant desires to remain comfortably warm, that it desires that it continue to be embraced, and that it desires that it continue to be nursed. But this is misleading because I do not think that the infant is aware that being warm, being embraced, and being nursed is the cause of its remaining in a comfortable state.

Desires and aversions similar to the infant's desire to remain comfortable are native desires and aversions. I do not know that it is only infants that experience native desires and aversions purely, that is, without being associated with other qualities. The infant desires natively the continuation of the comfortable feelings that accompany being embraced, and being nursed. These native desires, I imagine, are not very different from the native desires of any other newborn mammal. To begin, then, it is only these comfortable feelings that accompany being warm, being embraced, and being nursed that are desired by the typical infant. Also, it is only desired that these feelings be maintained while their being experienced. Infants do not desire that, in the future, these feelings reoccur. That would require, it seems, an understanding of the situation that the infant lacks. The infant does not desire anything of a general nature. It only is aware that, at the moment, it is either comfortable or uncomfortable. It desires to remain comfortable, and it desires not to remain uncomfortable.

Native desires are the simple desires we are born with. There are processes by which a person's desires are altered. Natively, an infant desires to remain comfortable, but later it becomes aware that it is comfortable when it is kept warm, embraced, and fed. By the Principle of Association, an infant can come to desire the more complex situation of being comfortable by being embraced by its mother. Only after the association is established is it possible for the infant to desire being embraced by its mother apart from the desire to remain comfortable. In fact, after the desire to be embraced by its mother becomes separate from the desire to remain comfortable, it is possible for the infant to acquire a desire to be embraced by its mother even if this regularly leads to discomfort.

Theories like Mill's can explain how masochists acquire the desire to be placed in painful situations. Masochism can be difficult to explain, given Psychological Hedonism. One might say that the masochist takes pleasure in painful situations, which seems odd. According to the association theory, the explanation of masochism is that natively the masochist is averse to all painful situations, but his peculiar desires have been acquired through association. Take the example of a person who desires to be spanked. We all expect painful sensations to occur as a result of being spanked. Many people can be conditioned to desire being spanked. The trick is initially to make the spanking less violent and to supplement the experience of being spanked with something that is actually desired, for instance, sexual stimulation. If the situation is repeated many times, each time making the spanking more violent and gradually eliminating the sexual stimulation, then the person can come to desire the spanking alone. Therefore, what is detested natively can become, by the application of Psychological Determinism and the Principle of Association, something that is desired.

Of all of the problems and questions raised by this discussion, the most pressing, given the topic of this essay, is that if Qualitative Utilitarianism were to be adopted then by what means could it be put into practice? In other words, assuming that those in power (in a democracy, the majority of the people) decided to adopt an ethical theory, then how would people be motivated to behave in the manner prescribed by the ethical theory? Mill's answer is that there exist (probably as native desires) "the social feelings of mankind." (<u>Utilitarianism</u>, p. 30) By the association of these feelings with the more definite program that follows from the theory, people can be directed towards the prescribed aims of utilitarianism.(16)

There is a serious gap in Mill's explanation, because the reliance on "social feelings" only works once a theory is adopted by those in power. If hedonistic utilitarianism is adopted by those in power then the masses can be conditioned to act so that the greatest happiness is produced. But what is there to motivate those in a position of power to adopt the theory? Having social feelings does not in itself lead one to utilitarianism as a philosophical view. Qualitative Utilitarianism is a good theory, and I believe that it should be implemented, but I am not holding that this belief can be explained merely by reference to a combination of my native desires, the Principle of Association, and Psychological Determinism. I presume that by studying Philosophy and by writing and reading essays, such as Mill's and mine, we have the capacity to assess and adopt these theories (to a great degree) independently of our historically founded psychological inclinations.

In a slightly different context, Mill anticipates this objection and gives what I find to be an unsatisfactory reply:

> The objectors to utilitarianism... say it is exacting too much to require that people shall always act from the inducement of promoting the general interest of society. But this is to mistake the very meaning of a standard of morals and confound the rule of action with the motive of it. (<u>Utilitarianism</u>, p. 17)

What I understand Mill to be saying is that the "rule of action", meaning the prescriptions of an ethical theory, is one thing and "the motive of it", meaning how it is that people are persuaded to act in accord with those prescriptions, is another. This is at odds

---

16. This is also the interpretation given by Berger in <u>Happiness, Justice, and Freedom</u>, pp. 19-23. Also see <u>Utilitarianism</u>, p. 30.

with the enlightened liberalism usually espoused by Mill, for a true liberal society is one where the people themselves recognize the legitimacy of a theory and adopt it of their own free choice. Mill seems to be saying that the populace should be blindly conditioned to the prescribed ends of utilitarianism. He seems to be holding that utilitarianism could flourish in a world of Psychological Egoists, given the right training. Even if the theory itself doesn't command their attention, Mill is saying that there do exist psychological tendencies within the general public that can be redirected to coincide with the aims of his theory.

Mill is caught between two traditions. His development of Qualitative Utilitarianism is a compromise between the harsh views of his acknowledged Benthamite predecessors and a newly-found enlightenment fostered by his friendship with Harriet Taylor and the influence of European humanists.(17)

Unfortunately, Mill has not yet tempered his psychological theory. He is still a Psychological Hedonist and a Psychological Determinist, and thus, he is compelled to explain how the populace can be influenced to act in accordance with his ethical theory, if it were proposed for adoption. At this point, Mill brings in the native tendency of being sympathetic to the plight of others. But given Psychological Hedonism, what explanation can be given for anyone in a position of authority holding that Mill's ethical theory ought to be adopted? It is unlikely that such a person (or group of people) would have a psychological history by which this theory had more of a positive association than any other theory. Thus, it can only accidentally happen that there exist an impetus in Mill's world of psychological hedonists that gets the ball rolling for a program to condition the general public to act in accordance with the aims of his ethical theory. Mill's psychological theory cannot explain how his ethical theory is to be adopted, and it is at odds with the other more liberal and progressive elements of his theory. My own view is that those in power are often able to judge the merits of an ethical theory freely and independently of their own inclination to pleasure,

---

17. See Chapters V. and VI. of Mill's Autobiography.

and it also seems that the public is capable of being convinced on rational grounds that they ought to accept a view proposed for adoption. Mill doesn't need Psychological Hedonism to uphold the major theses of his ethical theory, although he seems unaware of this. His empiricism with its appeal to experience is sufficient, as will be explained in the following chapter. Although Psychological Hedonism is not formally inconsistent with Qualitative Hedonism, it is incompatible with the liberalism of Qualitative Utilitarianism.

3. ETHICAL HEDONISM

A discussion of hedonism cannot go very far without making a distinction between Psychological Hedonism and Ethical Hedonism. Psychological Hedonism is a theory of motivation. According to it, nothing but the desire for pleasure moves people to action, or put in another way, human behavior can be explained by the relation between people and their quest for pleasure. Psychological Hedonism is not a normative theory. It neither praises nor condemns. Ethical Hedonism is a normative theory. According to it, people ought only to seek pleasure as an end, for it alone has intrinsic value. Psychological Hedonism is a theory used to explain how people are motivated. Ethical Hedonism is a theory that can be used to justify motivation directed towards pleasure.

Further distinctions are made relative to exactly who is or should be motivated by what particular pleasure. Egoistic Psychological Hedonism is the theory that a person is only motivated by the prospect of receiving pleasure for himself or herself. Universal Psychological Hedonism is the theory that people can only be motivated by the prospect of pleasure, but that the pleasure need not be their own, the prospect of others receiving pleasure also being a motivating factor. Under either version, if there are no prospects for anyone receiving pleasure from some action then there is no motivation for that action. Egoistic Ethical Hedonism and Universal Ethical Hedonism share a similar relation. According to the former, each individual ought to produce only his or her own pleasure. According to the latter, each individual ought to produce the most pleasure possible for everyone, not just pleasure for themselves. Universal Ethical Hedonism is equivalent to hedonistic utilitarianism without the consequentialistic element for according to the former, the greatest amount of pleasure taken over the greatest number of people is "the Good", and according to the latter, an action is right if and only if it results in the greatest possible amount of pleasure taken over the greatest number of people.

Psychological Hedonism and Ethical Hedonism are distinct theories. A Psychological Hedonist can consistently hold that it is a tragedy that people are only motivated by the desire for pleasure and wish that things were otherwise. An Ethical Hedonist can hold that some persons are in error by being motivated by something other than pleasure, and this is inconsistent with Psychological Hedonism. However, these two theories do complement one another with the application of the "ought implies can" principle.

According to the "ought implies can" principle, we are only morally obligated to perform actions that are possible to perform, or more simply, if you ought to act in some particular way then it follows that you can act in that particular way. For example, if Haley's Comet is on a path set directly towards The Earth then I am not morally obligated to stop it, even though a great deal of pain is to be expected when it arrives. Altering the course of the comet is not within the range of actions possible for me.

The name of the principle is misleading, because it implies that the relation between `ought´ and `can´ is of a logical nature. In the comet example, it is logically possible that I could alter the course of the comet. The description of the state-of-affairs in which I wish that the comet would turn on its course and then it does turn its course is consistent. It is even physically possible that I change the course of the comet, since no law of physics is violated by my construction of a device that exerted a force sufficient to alter the course of the comet. Yet, under the "ought implies can" principle, I am not obligated to alter the course of the comet because it is not practically possible for me to do so.

If one concept implies another then this is so either because of the logical structure of the concepts involved, as (A and B) implies B, or because of conceptual ties, like `the sky is blue´ implies `the sky is colored´. I find that the relation between `ought´ and `can´ is neither logical nor conceptual, but instead is founded on practical considerations. It is a difficult question. Someone might say, "I have reflected upon my understanding of the concept of being morally obligated to act in a particular way and I find within this concept (or somehow entailed by it) the concept of that action being possible for me to perform", and to this I can only reply that I find no such conceptual link.

Consider the following thought-experiment that seems to confirm my position. The inhabitants of Planet X are much like us, except that it is their nature to be deceiving and murderous derelicts. It is impossible for them to change. Are they morally obligated to change for the better? If they ought to change but could not do so, no matter how hard they tried, then it would be an immense tragedy. I can even imagine the finer citizens of Planet X realizing that they are moral degenerates and resolving to change, but in every case in which they are put in a tempting situation they revert to their old ways. My understanding of this thought-experiment is that there is some sense to the idea that the citizens are morally obligated to do what they cannot do. But from a strictly practical point of view, there is no point in holding that they ought to change, because there is no chance of this happening.

Therefore, I find the basis of the "ought implies can" principle to be more practical than philosophical. (18) I am not saying that philosophical questions are of little practical importance or that practical questions are of little philosophical importance. This is a question of the grounds of a principle, and I find that this principle lacks a basis within our most basic conceptual framework. Insofar as the subject of ethics is important as being influential upon our actions, we need only be concerned with the range of actions possible for us to perform, a range that I find to be of great dimensions. In the sense of `ought´ that demands compliance to some standard, it is of practical interest only to consider those obligations falling

---

18. For an opposing view, see Fred Wilson´s proof that "must implies ought" in "Mill´s Proof that Happiness is the Criterion of Morality", pp. 59-61.

within the range of possible alternative actions. Thus, I am holding that the "ought implies can" principle applies to ethics, but I do not think that the implication in this case is founded on anything other than practical considerations.

The affinity (and sometimes confusion) between Psychological Hedonism and Ethical Hedonism exists because, when taken with the "ought implies can" principle, Psychological Hedonism yields a conclusion similar to Ethical Hedonism. For the purposes of making this point, consider the following argument:

1. People can only seek pleasure [Psychological Hedonism].

which is equivalent to:

2. People cannot seek anything other than pleasure.

I here interpret the "ought implies can" principle as:

3. If people ought to seek something other than pleasure then they can seek something other than pleasure.

2. and 3. yield by <u>modus tollens</u>:

4. It is false that people ought to seek something other than pleasure.

Proposition 4. is not equivalent to Ethical Hedonism, but it does eliminate any other alternative except Ethical Nihilism, interpreted here as the position that no one is morally obligated in any way. So, we are left with:

5. If people ought to act in some way then that way can only be to seek pleasure.

I suspect that many Ethical Hedonists have arrived at their position by a reasoning process similar to that in the preceding argument. Jeremy Bentham, for example, seems to jump rather quickly from observing that, "Nature has placed mankind under the governance of two sovereign masters, <u>pain</u> and <u>pleasure</u>" to the conclusion that, "It is for them alone to point out what we ought to do."(19) This inference seems to

THE SENSATION THEORY OF PLEASURE

tacitly apply the "ought implies can" principle as explained in the preceding passages. Since I am rejecting Psychological Hedonism, in the following chapter "Qualitative Hedonism" I will be developing other arguments in support of Ethical Hedonism. I shall be later accepting a version of Psychological Hedonism, but on grounds very different from the apparently empirical grounds upon which Bentham and others founded their views.

4. THE SENSATION THEORY OF PLEASURE

Hedonism is defined as the theory that only pleasure has positive intrinsic value and only pain has negative intrinsic value. There are several ways that `pleasure´ and `pain´ might be defined, so there are several different interpretations of hedonism that vary according to what is understood to be signified by `pleasure´ and `pain´. In this section, I will examine several variations of the Sensation Theory of Pleasure. In the section to follow, I will examine the main alternative, the Desire Theory of pleasure.

I assume that pleasure is a psychological concept. Pleasure is not simply a type of behavior or a disposition towards some type of behavior.(20) That is not to say that pleasure is not closely related to behavior. Laughter and smiling are behaviors that usually occur in conjunction with the experience of pleasure. Also, it is true that we are disposed to act in particular ways because of pleasure (or escape from pain) we expect to receive. Yet, careful introspection clearly shows that there is an essential factor in pleasant experiences that cannot be adequately accounted for

---

19. Paragraph I. of Chapter I. of An Introduction to the Principles of Morals and Legislation.

20. This argument is taken from Edwards´ Pleasures and Pains, pp. 26-29. One might suppose that Gilbert Ryle held that pleasure is a disposition, as was his way of dealing with other mental concepts. He also rejects the Sensation Theory, and instead, his position is that pleasure is a variety of "heed". See The Concept of Mind, pp.132-133 and Penelhum´s "The Logic of Pleasure", pp. 489-497.

THE SENSATION THEORY OF PLEASURE

merely by descriptions limited to behavior. The proof of this assertion rests on an appeal to personal experience. There a difference between behavior associated with pleasure that includes the intimate enjoyment factor and behavior without it. For various reasons, people sometimes pretend to be enjoying themselves when really they are not. This is especially true in the case of actors on the stage. They sometimes behave exactly as if they were experiencing pleasure. If, from personal experience, you find that there is an important difference between behaving as if you were experiencing pleasure and actually experiencing pleasure then you know that pleasure is not just a type of behavior.

For similar reasons, pleasure is not simply a disposition to behave in a particular way.(21) It is true that if sleeping late is pleasurable for me then I will tend to behave that way. Generally, people tend to behave in ways that produce pleasure for them. But in saying, "Smith is enjoying the party", it is implied that a psychological event is occurring...Smith's personally enjoying the party. If Smith passes out then he is unconscious and is no longer capable of enjoying the party, even though it is still true that Smith loves parties and is still disposed to attend them. So, the pleasure of party participation and the disposition to attend parties are not the same.

Without getting too deeply involved in problems within the philosophy of mind, it seems safe to assume that the meaning of `pleasure´ and `pain´ is tied to a type of psychological episode that occurs in the mental life of conscious beings. A psychological episode is simply a temporal part of the mental life

---

21. Penelhum defines a dispositional concept as a statement that "does not make a categorical assertion to the effect that any episode, public or private, is occurring, but uses a linguistic device for making a definite or indefinite set of hypothetical statements about what that thing or person would do if certain circumstances obtained." ("The Logic of Pleasure", p. 497. For additional arguments opposed to the episodic view of pleasure, see Quinn's "Pleasure---Disposition or Episode?".

of a person. Actually, our experience is fairly continuous. There are usually no boundaries that separate discrete psychological episodes. My attending a party and the pleasure that occurs in that time period run into my walking home in the rain and the displeasure that takes place during that time period. But, for present purposes, there is nothing misleading about treating my attending the party as an episode separate from my walking home.

A conscious person is simply an ordinary person who is currently aware of some of his or her own mental processes. An unconscious person is not aware, and since pleasure is a type of (or part of a) mental process, then an unconscious person is not capable of experiencing pleasure. The Sensation Theory defines pleasure as being a type of sensation. It follows from this theory that pleasures are found to have properties similar to other sensations. As is true of other sensations, for pleasures their <u>esse est percipi</u>. This has two implications. Pleasures exist only when they are being experienced, and the nature of each pleasure is made fully manifest in the episode in which it is experienced.

There are no unconscious pleasures. If pleasure is experienced while sleeping then the person experiencing the pleasure must be conscious (to some degree) at that time. This is opposed to Plato's view that there are false pleasures (22), that is, events that seem pleasant but are really only the cessation of pain, as in the case of the moron who bangs his head against the wall because it feels so good when he stops. It seems pleasant when he stops, but all that really occurs, on Plato's view, is the cessation of pain. If the <u>esse est percipi</u> principle holds, then those who hold the Sensation Theory are committed to the position that if it seems pleasant to the moron then a pleasant episode actually occurs when he stops banging his head.

Conscious persons experience several different kinds of psychological episodes. An important question

---

22. <u>Philebus</u> 37a. Penelhum argues in a similar way against Plato's view in "The Logic of Pleasure", pp. 499-500.

THE SENSATION THEORY OF PLEASURE

that different theories of pleasure attempt to answer is, "How do we separate the episodes that are pleasures and pains from those that are not?" There are two main views on this question, the Sensation Theory and the Desire Theory. The former theory is based on something similar to the position that C.D. Broad calls the "tripartite division" of the mind, which "subdivides all mental events into Cognitions, Conations, and Feelings"(23) (the latter being equivalent to what I am calling `sensations´). Sensations are defined by their immediacy and lack of an intentional object. They are like a tickle or cold chill that seems to run up the spine, immediately present to the mind and neither needing nor admitting of any interpretation. Unlike cognitions, sensations do not take an object. I think about the chair, but I do not sense (in the narrow meaning of the word) about anything. We have all experienced sensations that were pleasant. A non-circular definition of pleasure within the category of sensation is that it is a type of sensation that we usually wish to continue. (24) There are two alternatives that arise at this point. Either pleasure is a single type of sensation or pleasure covers several types of sensation. I´ll call the former the `Homogeneous Sensation Theory´ and the latter the `Heterogeneous Sensation Theory´.

The Homogeneous Sensation Theory is more widely held by philosophers than the Heterogeneous Sensation Theory. The distinction is often disregarded, which amounts to adopting the homogeneous theory. Nevertheless, careful introspection shows that the homogeneous theory is false. If I find drinking a glass of wine to be pleasant and if I find that taking a swim on a hot day to be a pleasant then, according to the Homogeneous Sensation Theory, the same type of sensation occurs in in both episodes. What if I drink a glass of wine while I am in the pool? If pleasures are what they seem to

----

23. <u>Five Types of Ethical Theory</u>, pp. 228-229. Broad does not advocate the Sensation Theory, for he finds that pleasure falls under both the sensation and the cognition categories.

24. This is similar to Sidgwick´s definition in <u>A Method of Ethics</u>, pp. 42-43.

THE SENSATION THEORY OF PLEASURE

be, and if these seem to be different types of sensations, then the Homogeneous Sensation Theory is false. Also, people often desire a variety of pleasant activities. If there is only one type of pleasant sensation, and if it alone is desired, then it is unlikely that people would prefer a variety of pleasant experiences to a single type of experience that regularly provided them with pleasure.

Finally, enjoying one type of pleasant sensation often interrupts the activity involved in enjoying some other type of pleasant sensation. The pleasures of marksmanship are incompatible with the sudden sensation of pleasure from some other activity. The second sensation of pleasure disallows the concentration necessary for the enjoyment of sharpshooting. If pleasure is a single type of sensation then the pleasure of one activity should not interfere with the pleasure of another activity.

There is a further distinction that can be made within the Sensation Theory. Pleasure may be simply identified with a type of sensation (homogeneous or heterogeneous) or there is the option to make the occurrence of a pleasant sensation a necessary condition for identifying a psychological episode as being a pleasure. The difference between these two theories is that in the first, `pleasure´ refers to only a pleasant sensation, and in the second, `pleasure´ refers to a complex psychological event of which a pleasant sensation is a component. To keep things in order, I´ll call the first theory the `Simple´ theory and the second, the `Component´ theory.

Thus, there are four distinct theories within the Sensation Theory of pleasure:

1. The Simple Homogeneous Sensation Theory,

2. The Component Homogeneous Sensation Theory,

3. The Simple Heterogeneous Sensation Theory, and

4. The Component Heterogeneous Sensation Theory.

On phenomenological grounds and from observations of behavior, I have rejected the two homogeneous theories. Thus, we are left with the two heterogeneous theories.

The apparent advantage of the Simple theory (in each of its forms) is its precision, and I suppose that this is the main reason for its popularity. If the tripartite (or some similar) division of mental events is held then to identify `pleasure´ with one type of sensation ties down the concept very neatly. Initially, there seems to be no great problem with adopting the Simple Theory, but it surely is not in accord with the usual understanding of the meaning of `pleasure´. When we speak of pleasures, *e.g.*, the pleasure of going swimming this afternoon, we usually are referring to the entire psychological episode associated with the activity of swimming. There are rare exceptions. One lover may say to another, "I really feel pleasure at this moment", and, in this type of case, `pleasure´ might only signify a sensation and not the entire episode. I would say, to be more precise, the lover should say, I really feel an intensely pleasant sensation at this moment, which still qualifies the episode as being a pleasure under the Component Theory, since the episode has a pleasant sensation as a component. The Heterogeneous Component Theory accomodates references to pleasure sensations, but the Heterogeneous Simple Theory cannot accomodate common usage when we mean to refer to the entire experience. Therefore, of the sensation theories, the Component Heterogeneous Sensation theory seems to coincide best with the phenomenological data and our ordinary understanding of the concept of pleasure.

5. PLEASURE AND DESIRE

The Desire Theory of pleasure is the main alternative to the Sensation Theory. Within the Desire Theory, pleasure is defined as being the intentional object of desire, and pain is defined as being the intentional object of detesting (or aversion). There are several ways to develop the Desire Theory, depending on the philosophy of mind and the definitions of pleasure, pain, desire and aversion one adopts. Within the theory I am here developing, there is an interesting analogy between desiring, thinking, and their respective objects, pleasures and ideas.

At this point, the definition is neutral in regard to the question of whether or not pleasures and ideas are exclusively psychological entities. The question is, "Can I only desire or think of things that exist

PLEASURE AND DESIRE

dependently on my mind?" For example, Am I desiring or thinking of only my idea of the girl next door, or am I really desiring or thinking of her as she exists independently of my mind? No matter what the status of their objects may be, desiring and thinking are each a type of psychological episode, and each has its own kind of intentional object. Desiring is not merely feeling desire. Careful introspection reveals that desiring has an intentional object much like that of thinking.

It seems plausible to hold that no intelligible account of either thinking or ideas can be given without reference to the other. It's not the most precise definition, but I might well define `thinking´ as a type of mental activity and `ideas´ as those things we think about. In a similar vein, I observe that there are psychological episodes in which persons are engaged in the mental activity desiring and when this activity occurs there exists an object of the mental activity, the pleasure. Often, come Friday evening, I desire to drink a bottle of wine with friends. I am the person, the type of mental event is desire, and drinking the wine taken with the company of friends is the pleasure to which the mental event is directed. These are paradigm cases in which actual persons are engaged in the mental activity of actually desiring some object, which the Desire Theory defines as the pleasure to which the mental activity is directed. Events of this sort are not uncommon. An infant desires the pleasure associated with cuddling its mother, students desire the pleasures that follow from scholastic achievement, and workers desire the pleasure of spending their paychecks.

Since the actual mental events of persons desiring pleasures are not the only instances of pleasure, we cannot simply define pleasure as the intentional object of an actual case of desiring. Not all pleasures are intentional objects of actual desires. I desire to own a farm. I occasionally engage in the mental activity of desiring to own a farm, when driving in the country looking at a particular farm. In these cases, it is a particular farm and I am actually desiring it. If I am engaged in the activity of desiring to own a farm and it is not the desire for any particular farm, but rather, simply the desire to own a nice little farm, then the desire is actual and the pleasure is more

PLEASURE AND DESIRE

general. Of course, I do not desire to own a possible farm. That would be like having imaginary money to spend. Rather, I am desiring to own any one of several different farms that have the potential of satisfying this desire.

An actual event of my desiring to own some particular farm only scratches the surface of my desire to own a nice, little farm. I am not engaged in the mental activity of desiring to own a farm twenty four hours a day. It seems correct to say that I desire to own a farm during the time I am studying, teaching, eating, and sleeping, even though I am not actually experiencing that desire. If all that I desired were that which I was actually desiring at any given moment then I could only desire one thing (or possibly a few things) at any one time. But I have many different desires over an extended length of time, and it seems that so does everyone else. Thus, not all desires are desires that actually occur, and likewise, pleasures are not limited to merely being the objects of occurrent desires.

The meaning of pleasure and desire is primarily known by experience of actual cases of desiring some particular pleasure. Basic to our knowledge of desire are particular experiences of desiring, and basic to our knowledge of pleasures is what we have actually found to be pleasant. Any definition of pleasure and desire that is limited to actual cases is too narrow. Yet, on the other hand, any definition of pleasure and desire that excludes cases of actually desiring some actual pleasurable object excludes the cases that are best known to be instances of pleasure and desire. In some cases, confronting the pleasure stimulates the desire and in other cases the order is reversed. There are many things that I would find to be the object of my desire if I were confronted with them,. There are many situations such that if I were to be placed in them, a desire would surface.

Therefore, within this version of the Desire Theory of pleasure, the nature of `desire´ and `pleasure´ (and similarly, `detest´ and `pain´) is best expressed by a definition that contains subjunctives. `Pleasure´ is either what is desired or what would be desired, given the proper situation. `Desire´ is a species of mental activity focused towards a given pleasure or is a species of mental activity that would be focused toward that pleasure given the proper situation. In the case of my desiring to own a small farm, it is either an occurrent experience of wanting the farm or, as is the case in which I come across the right farm while on a drive through the country, I would experience the desire, given that situation.

By "desire" I mean only those conscious experiences of a person aware that he or she is desiring and aware of what he or she is desiring, or in the case of dispositions to desire, the person would be aware of the desire if it occurred. Possibly, unconscious but occurrent desires exist, but they are of little concern within the context of ethics. Issues of what is `right´ focus upon the impact on world events of actions in relation to the conscious desires of persons. If a person consciously desires something, then it is a pleasure to him or her, and there are **prima facie** grounds for it being right to act so that this particular person´s desires be satisfied (and similarly, that a person´s pains be averted) This is the point at which utilitarianism has a humanistic basis. If a person has an unconscious desire then there are no such grounds.

Jan Narveson in **Morality** and **Utility** (pp. 75-76) discusses a common approach to the definition of pleasures---that they are the **satisfaction** of our desires. This is not much different from my defining pleasure and pain as being the intentional objects of of the mentality of desire and aversion. I have argued that the scope of pleasure is too narrow if we confine it to actual cases of being the object of one´s desires, and that we must allow those objects that would be an object of desire, given the proper situation. Likewise, to define pleasure as being the satisfaction of desires is too narrow, since it limits pleasures to being only the occurrent episodes in which desires are satisfied. Many things are pleasures in that they have the potential of being satisfying. As utilitarians, we seek to produce the maximum pleasure possible. This pleasure is not occurrently satisfying any desire, but we hope it will. Satisfaction is the basis for the value of pleasure, not the pleasure itself. Pleasure is the intentional object of a desiring mentality, which is primarily those things and properties that are the focus of that mentality, which are the phenomenological objects of that mentality, for example, the girl next door, an ice cream bar, or a college degree. We desire satisfaction only secondarily, depending on our belief that situations in which we have access to pleasures will be satisfying.

The preceding point relates to another question, that being if there is value only in the satisfaction of "rational" desires. A necessary, but not sufficient, condition for a desire being rational is that the person who is desiring is conscious of that desire. Richard Brandt, in A Theory of the Right and the Good (p. 156), defines "irrational desires" as follows:

> Irrational desires are very similar to inchoherent beliefs and conditioned but unjustified fears. If we survey types of irrational desires...they are desires which develop from the artificial process of culture transmission...or from unfortunate experiences during childhood...By definition `irrational´ desires are one and all ones that the person would lose if he repeatedly reminded himself of known facts about himself or the world.

Brandt´s definition is a good start, but seems to admit cases which I find to be clearly `irrational´. At the extreme, if a mad scientist "repeatedly reminded himself" of his own diabolical nature and of the fact that he might destroy the world, and if the desire to destroy the world were not abated, it does not follow that this is a rational desire. The desires of an obese person who has been through several weight reduction programs qualify as rational on Brant´s criteria, and yet, they are not rational if they lead to poor health and self-destruction. My own view is that rational desires are those desires conducive to the happiness of the individual and conducive to the happiness of others affected by the actions of the individual. The detailed knowledge of which desires are rational comes only through experience, a topic covered in the next chapter.

According to the Desire Theory, there is no difference between what is a pleasure to a person and what is desired by that person or what would be desired by that person if confronted with it. Therefore, that only pleasure is desired follows from the definition of pleasure and desire within the Desire Theory of pleasure, because a person's pleasures are those things that either he is desiring or those things that would be desired by him if he were confronted with them. Hence, nothing can be desired but pleasure. Thus, to say that only pleasure is desired means that only what can be desired by a person is desired by that person, and so, if we assume that we can do only what we desire to do, Psychological Hedonism is necessarily true. On the other hand, a Psychological Hedonist holding the Sensation theory could hold that it is a contingent truth based upon biological fact that people only desire pleasure sensations, and that if our biological nature was changed then we might desire some other type of sensation.

To know that only pleasure is desired does not tell us specifically what each individual actually desires. There are similarities between what is desired or would be desired from individual to individual, but since humans have such diverse personalities, their desires will differ greatly for reasons both physical and psychological. I have observed that there is no single thing that is universally desired, and thus, any proposition of the form, `all persons desire _____´ is false. Exceptions are the vacuous `all persons desire only what they can desire´, and the `all persons only desire pleasure´ (so defined). It is false that all persons desire self-preservation because some people act on the desire for self-destruction. It is false that all persons desire to eat, to sleep, and to escape the cold because there are cases of people acting on the desire to starve, to stay awake, and to catch cold. It is false that all persons desire any particular sensation, although most people desire those sensations often called `pleasure´, because some people desire those sensations which the majority finds aversive and calls `pain´.

If there is nothing that is universally desired, then there is no simple quality that defines pleasure. Thus, if pleasure is to be defined, it must be defined by some other means. If there were a simple quality that defines pleasure then there would be a quality by which pleasures, taken in themselves, could be identified conceptually, rather than enumeratively. All particular pleasures can be identified insofar as, if we were to become aware of them in the right circumstances, they would be desired, but the point here is that they cannot be identified apart from that relation.

No two individuals desire exactly the same collection of things. Any individual can come to desire almost anything. What might mislead us to think otherwise is the observation that there are some things that are generally, but not universally, desired, and so they have come to be called `pleasures´. All experiences of eating sweets are not pleasures, because the experience of eating sweets is not pleasant for everyone. There are sensations that are commonly desired, and sometimes these are referred to as `pleasures´. But there are cases when these sensations are neither actually nor potentially desired. When this is the case, then in relation to that person, those sensations, are not, as defined by the Desire Theory, pleasures for that person.

In a sense, thinking is superior to desiring, because thinking about something usually gives a clearer picture and more accurate information about its intentional object than desiring. My desire to drink a glass of water doesn´t tell me much about the water, except that I find water to be desirable. When I am in the state of desiring the water I am not especially concerned with the details about the water, I simply desire it. You can be fully aware of your desiring some object and yet have almost no understanding of the nature of the object. But thinking about some object is almost always accompanied by some understanding of the object. If I think about the water, I think about it as being a clear liquid contained in the glass, situated on the table. I think of the water evaporating off the surface of the ocean, forming clouds, blowing in, and eventually, filling the city reservoir and flowing to the faucet. I might also think deeper about the chemical bonds between the oxygen atom and the two hydrogen atoms.

Even though thinking is superior to desiring in the respect of leading to an understanding of the nature of the intentional object, not all that is known by desiring the object can be appreciated by merely thinking about the object. Thus, that I desire X informs me of my relation to X in a way that cannot be totally understood merely by my thinking of X. If "the

PLEASURE AND DESIRE

Good" is defined by reference to desirability, then without knowing what is most desirable for me I cannot know what is good for me. It is likely that things that resemble things that are desirable to me would also be desirable, and in this respect thinking can inform of what is desirable to me. If I have actually desired chocolate milk shakes, then it is likely that I will find chocolate cakes desirable, and this can be known through the thinking process. But at the heart of it remains desiring, and I am claiming that knowing my desires is an essential element of my knowing what is good for me, or anyone else's knowing what is good for me. If "the Good" is a species of "the desired" then some knowledge of "the desired" is a necessary condition for knowledge of "the Good". Understanding "the desired" requires having some experience of desiring. Thus, some experience of desiring is a necessary condition for knowing about "the Good", given the above assumptions. Thus, there is an interesting epistemological connection between the Desire Theory of Pleasure and the Desire Theory of "the Good".

I have not proved that the Desire Theory is superior to the Sensation Theory of pleasure. My conclusion is that, taken apart from their relation to ethics (to be discussed in the next chapter), there is no clear conclusion. I prefer the Desire Theory over the Heterogeneous Sensation Theory of pleasure, but there seems to be no evidence, taken apart from normative theories, that conclusively shows that the Desire Theory is correct. The Sensation Theory offers the promise of precision and scientific credibility. The Desire Theory is more compatible with ordinary language and phenomenological considerations.

In the following chapter, I argue that the ethical theory most compatible with the Sensation Theory of Pleasure leads to absurd consequences, and that an ethical theory most compatible with the Desire Theory is most plausible. If I am correct about this then an important issue in the philosophy of mind is settled by evidence based on ethical theory, and this is most peculiar. However, philosophers should be able to tie together the findings of several areas within the field, and they might also rely on the findings in one area to clarify problems in another.

CHAPTER THREE

QUALITATIVE HEDONISM

1. QUANTITATIVE HEDONISM

Hedonism is the view that only pleasure has intrinsic ethical value. Quantitative Hedonism is a theory about how different pleasures are to be evaluated. According to it, each pleasure and pain can be assigned a numerical value, with a greater quantity of pleasure over pain always being preferable to a lesser quantity of pleasure over pain. I further define Quantitative Hedonism as making no distinctions in the evaluation of the pleasure and pain over and above the following three factors:

1. The intensity of the pleasure or pain,

2. The duration of the pleasure or pain, and

3. The effect of the episode in which pleasure or pain occurs in relation to subsequent pleasures and pains.

Qualitative Hedonism is defined negatively as being any hedonistic theory of evaluation other than Quantitative Hedonism. So, if a hedonistic theory makes distinctions such that they are a significant departure from the above three factors then it is Qualitative Hedonism.

The intensity of a pleasure or pain is simply the magnitude of the pleasure or pain insofar as it is felt (or sensed) by the person experiencing the pleasure or pain. Pleasure is assigned a positive magnitude, pain a negative magnitude. Pains of a high magnitude seem to be more common than highly intense pleasures. For example, the pain of hitting my thumb with a hammer last week was of a very high magnitude, probably of a higher magnitude than the intensity of any pleasure I experienced in the last week. An example of a pleasure of a low magnitude is the pleasure taken in a drive through the countryside. I had a pleasant drive the other day, but at no time was the pleasure very intense.

An indication of the magnitude of a pleasure or pain is the degree to which it commands our attention. The pain from hitting my thumb last week was so intense that, at the time, I could think of nothing else. The pleasure of the drive through the countryside was less intense. I was able to pay attention to the task of driving my automobile. The attention that intense pleasures or pains command can cause a person to act in an unusually irrational manner. For example, having caught fire, people sometimes panic and run and so, fan the flames instead of rolling on the ground to put them out. It is dangerous to drive with the radio playing loudly, because the pleasure of listening can interfere with driving.

The measurement of the intensity of pleasure and pain is not strictly objective. Pleasures and pains can only be quantified ordinally in respect to one another. The most pleasurable or painful experience possible rates a `10´ (or whatever scale you wish to begin with) and the barest perceptible pleasure or pain rates a small fraction. Variations in intensity are possible within a single episode. In the case of hitting my thumb with a hammer, the initial intensity of pain was `~8´ and it diminished to `0´ at an even rate over a span of fifteen minutes. The intensity of the experience can be defined by the average intensity of the pain taken over the duration of the episode, in this case a `~4´. The most exciting moment in the drive through the countryside was spotting a deer, a `+4´. Overall, the drive had an average intensity of `+2´.

The duration factor is simply the magnitude of the time period over which the pleasant or painful experience occurs. When I smashed my thumb, the pain lasted about fifteen minutes, so the duration is quantified as `15´. The drive through the countryside lasted for a half-hour, so its duration is `30´. Unlike intensity, the duration factor has an objective basis. The duration of a pleasurable or painful experience that lasts fifteen minutes for me is quantified by the same criterion as a pleasurable or painful experience that lasts fifteen minutes for anyone else.

Thus, according to this approach, each pleasurable or painful psychological episode, taken in itself, can be quantified by taking the arithmetic product of the intensity and duration factors. The episode of my hitting my thumb last week had an average intensity of ~4 multiplied by a duration of 15, which yields ~60 hedonic units. The drive through the countryside had an average intensity of +2 multiplied by a duration of 30,

QUANTITATIVE HEDONISM

which yields +60 hedonic units. An episode can be composed of a mixture of positive and negative hedonic units. If the pleasures of my drive were interupted by a five minute toothache of a ~5 intensity then the episode would still have 25 minutes of +2 intensity, and the total would be +50 units less the ~25 units for the toothache which amounts to +25 hedonic units.

The idea that a pleasant experience can be evaluated merely by taking the product of the average intensity of the pleasure experienced and duration of the experience is most compatible with the Sensation Theory of pleasure, since sensations are more easily quantified in terms of intensity and durations than the objects of desires. But supporting the Desire Theory is the experience that many episodes that are clearly pleasant lack a clear indication of intensity. There is also a difference between the overall intensity of an experience and the intensity of pleasures that occur within it. The intensity of an experience largely depends on the attention it demands of us. It is generally true that the occurrence of highly intense pleasure and pain sensations grab our attention, but there are situations that both demand attention and lack these sensations. Sudden danger demands our attention, as in the case of narrowly escaping an automobile accident. Concentrating on a philosophical issue demands attention, but need not be accompanied by pleasant or painful sensations. Evaluation of the intensity of a pleasant experience with only reference to the intensity of the pleasure sensation presupposes the Sensation Theory of pleasure, because the other components of the experience are disregarded. A drive through the countryside can be quite pleasant while having no clear pleasure sensation component that can be easily quantified.

Likewise, if pleasure is only a sensation then it has a definite duration, because all sensations have a definite duration. Pleasure as defined by the Desire Theory does not always lend itself to definition in respect to duration. Suppose I have owned a small farm that was and continues to be a pleasure to me for one year. Should I quantify the pleasure as having a duration of exactly 365 days? This seems to place an inordinate value on that pleasure. Often, under the Desire Theory, the duration of pleasures is indefinite. The idea that pleasure has a definite duration is most compatible with the Sensation Theory. If so, then the plausibility of Quantitative Hedonism depends on (and falls with) the plausibility of the Sensation Theory of pleasure.

The third and final factor for assessing the value of pleasures and pains is the effect of the pleasurable or painful episode in relation to subsequent pleasures and pains. Both the effects for the person experiencing the pleasure and the effects in relation to other people are counted. The episode that includes the pleasures of my consuming alcoholic beverages last night cannot be properly evaluated without taking into account the pain of the hangover of the morning after, and, more generally, the effects of my drinking in relation to the pleasures and pains of other people. The future pleasure taken in reading poetry that is expected to result from studying poetry this evening should be taken into account when evaluating that activity. The main effect that followed hitting my thumb with the hammer last week is that it is less likely that I will hit my thumb again in the future because I will be careful to avoid the repetition of that painful experience. The positive effects of my being more careful in the future lowers the negative hedonic value of the experience from ~60 units to approximately ~50 units.

The philosophy of Jeremy Bentham as stated in his An Introduction to the Principles of Morals and Legislation (Chapter IV, Paragraphs III and IV) contains the classic statement of Quantitative Hedonism. There he lists seven "circumstances" that are to be applied in the evaluation of a pleasant or painful psychological episode. They are:

>   1. Its intensity.
>   2. Its duration.
>   3. Its certainty or uncertainty.
>   4. Its propinquity or remoteness.
>   5. Its fecundity.
>   6. Its purity.
>   And...
>   7. Its extent; that is, the number of persons...who are affected by it.

Since I am claiming that Quantitative Hedonism relies on only three factors, intensity, duration, and effect,

QUANTITATIVE HEDONISM

and since Bentham lists seven factors, an explanation is due. Bentham´s first two factors, intensity and duration, are identical to mine.

Bentham´s third and fourth factors, "certainty" (with its opposite, "uncertainty") and "propinquity" (including it opposite, "remoteness"), are founded on considerations that apply equally to Quantitative Hedonism and Qualitative Hedonism, and so, their function within Bentham´s theory does not constitute a departure from Quantitative Hedonism. The certainty factor only applies to anticipated pleasures, for once a pleasure has occurred, it is no longer a matter of probability. It either has or has not occurred. This is simply common sense. From a hedonistic viewpoint, a chance of experiencing a pleasure is never as desirable as the certainty of experiencing a pleasure of equal value, no matter if the evaluation follows quantitative or qualitative methods. A pleasure that will be experienced in the distant future has, on the face of it, as much value as one that will be experienced in the near future. Of course, often an anticipated future pleasure is less likely to occur, simply for the reason that the farther into the future we make our projections, the less likely it is that we will be correct about them, but certainty, the third factor, takes care of that. Therefore, the propinquity factor is based solely on the human characteristic of impatience and this can be applied equally well to a quantitative or qualitative theory.

Bentham´s fifth, sixth, and seventh factors, fecundity, purity, and extent, are all merely elaborations on effect, my third factor, and thus, his theory remains within the bounds of Quantitative Hedonism. Bentham defines fecundity and purity as follows:

> 5. Its <u>fecundity</u>, or the chance it has of being followed by sensations of the <u>same</u> kind: that is, pleasures, if it be a pleasure: pains, if it be a pain.
>
> 6. Its <u>purity</u>, or the chance it has of not being followed by sensations of the <u>opposite</u> kind: that is, pains, if it be a pleasure: pleasures, if it be a pain.

CRITIQUE OF QUANTITATIVE UTILITARIANISM

Fecundity, then, is the effect of a pleasant or painful experience producing a like experience in the future. The pleasant experience of first tasting a good wine develops a tendency to choose that wine again in the future, and so, the first experience causes (to some degree) further similar pleasures to occur in the future. The purity factor is the opposite of the fecundity factor. The purity of a pleasure is its tendency not to produce future pains. In the wine example, if the initial pleasures of tasting a good wine leads to displeasures of overconsumption then the experience lacks purity. "Extent", Bentham's final factor, also falls under my effect factor, for it is, by definition, the effect of the pleasant or painful psychological episode on other persons. Without the extent factor, Bentham's theory could be egoistic instead of utilitarian, for the other six factors are compatible with Ethical Egoism. We may conclude that Bentham's theory is an example of Quantitative Utilitarianism.

2. CRITIQUE OF QUANTITATIVE UTILITARIANISM

Practical (and perhaps, logical) problems of the measurement of pleasure and pain cause difficulties for Quantitative Hedonism. These problems stem from the privacy and ultimate subjectivity of pleasures and pains. However, I see the most important objection to Quantitative Hedonism as being the absurdity of its practical implications. In a similar vein, John Stuart Mill recounts a typical reaction to hedonism in the second chapter of Utilitarianism (p. 7):

> To suppose that life has (as they express it) no higher end than pleasure--no better and nobler object of desire and pursuit--they designate as utterly mean and groveling, as a doctrine only worthy of swine...

The development of Qualitative Hedonism in Utilitarianiam is Mill's reply to the above objection, which is seen by him as only pertaining to Quantitative Hedonism. To say that hedonism is a doctrine only fit for swine is a way of saying that the practical implications of hedonism are absurd. Mill's development of Qualitative Hedonism gives us a doctrine that more closely coincides with our (supposedly) nobler visions of human life.

CRITIQUE OF QUANTITATIVE UTILITARIANISM

All of this raises two questions. FIRST, what are the practical implications of Quantitative Hedonism? And SECOND, do these implications make the theory obviously implausible? There are two interpretations of Quantitative Hedonism in regard to the first question that are at opposite extremes, and so, I suppose that the truth lies somewhere between them. One I shall call the "Pleasure Center Interpretation", the other, the "Reduction Interpretation". The second question will be answered through an examination of these two interpretations.

In order to examine the practical implications of Quantitative hedonism, I shall look at Quantitative Utilitarianism, the most common way of applying Quantitative Hedonism to ethical issues. According to Quantitative Utilitarianism, of the alternative actions available to us, the right one is the one that produces the greatest amount of pleasure possible. The Pleasure Center Interpretation of the theory describes a situation that, if realized, results in the most efficient production of pleasure (evaluated quantitatively) possible.

The first point that leads towards the Pleasure Center Interpretation is that it is unlikely that pleasure can be maximized in a natural setting. By "natural" I mean without direct stimulation of pleasure by chemicals, surgical techniques, or electrical devices. A problem for Quantitative Utilitarians is that in a natural setting, the experience of pleasure is limited by complicated psychological systems that are not fully understood, and so, are not easily controlled. We are all subject to guilt and other hindrances to experiencing as much pleasure as we might. Even in the most pleasant environment possible, a hotel on a sandy beach in Hawaii, for example, most people find a reason to become somewhat dissatisfied and so, limit their enjoyment of pleasure.

A massive program of artificial pleasure stimulation would not be practical in the present circumstances. People undergoing continual, intense experiences of pleasure while in private homes and at their present places of employment would make homes, highways and factories unsafe. As is often true of drug addicts, people would be unable to care for their physical needs when in such a state. The solution

CRITIQUE OF QUANTITATIVE UTILITARIANISM

proposed by the Pleasure Center Interpretation is to build giant complexes where people are stimulated to continually experience pleasure in a safe, controlled environment. Of course, a few people would need to be "straight" part of the time in order to maintain the pleasure centers and the outside production of goods necessary to keep the system going. Ideally, from the perspective of the Quantitative Utilitarian, these would be people who for some biological reason would be unable to sustain long-term intensely pleasurable experiences.

Once the pleasure centers are established, the needs of its residents will be quite simple. A coffin-like box with electrical pleasure stimulators attached to surgically placed terminals, tubes supplying a mixture of watered-down mush and drugs, and a sanitary shower spray with drain would suffice. I can picture thousands stacked high in giant warehouses with a skeleton crew carefully monitoring gauges that warn of any malfunction. Outside of the Pleasure Center, some agriculture and manufacturing activity would be necessary to supply raw materials, but robots and automation would minimize the number of persons denied a place at the pleasure center.

Philosophers should be careful not to dismiss too quickly an implication of an otherwise plausible theory as being absurd or implausible. The idea of government based upon the "one man, one vote" principle might have easily seemed absurd to a medieval thinker. I find the idea of establishing pleasure centers to be patently absurd, even though I am trying to appreciate all the pleasure and lack of pain that would be created by them. There would be no wars, for everyone would be totally preoccupied with the experience of pleasure. There would be no need to build universities, museums, or parks. Yet, it is highly unlikely that anyone would advocate such a scheme. Thus, if the Pleasure Center Interpretation is correct then there are grounds for dismissing Quantitative Utilitarianism, for it leads to these absurd implications.

At the other extreme is the Reduction Interpretation. According to it, when the fecundity factor is duly applied, there is little practical difference between adopting Quantitative or Qualitative Utilitarianism. What are classified as higher pleasures in

CRITIQUE OF QUANTITATIVE UTILITARIANISM

the latter are accounted for as being pleasures of high fecundity in the former. The increased value of the higher pleasures as defined in qualitative theory is claimed by those holding the Reduction Interpretation to be handled by taking account of their fecundity and purity. For example, the higher pleasures of aesthetic appreciation, as defined by the qualitative theory, are also held in high esteem by the quantitative theory, since aesthetic appreciation has purity---it does not have a tendency to produce displeasure as an after-effect, and aesthetic appreciation has fecundity---it leads to the experience of similar pleasures in the future.

The practical implications of Qualitative Utilitarianism are quite dissimilar to the Pleasure Center Interpretation, and instead call for promoting the higher pleasures by creating a society that fosters the appreciation of the Arts, Nature, Literature. (See pp. 128-131 for more on this topic.) There is a problem, though, if it is also possible to artifically stimulate the higher pleasures. If so, then the practical implications of Qualitative Utilitarianism will more closely resemble those of the Quantitative Utilitarianism. I do find the idea of thousands of people lying in their pleasure boxes enjoying the pleasures of studying Philosophy and appreciating great works of Art preferable to the consequences of the Pleasure Center Interpretation. I cannot rule out the possibility of the artificial stimulation of higher pleasures, if Psychological Parallelism is true. If so, then there is a physical state that corresponds to each psychological state, and it is theoretically possible to stimulate a person into any physical state by artificial methods. That higher pleasures take an intentional object also does not rule out the possibility of artificial stimulation, since intentionality is a phenomenologically based concept, and so, the enjoyment of the intentional objects of higher pleasures is possible even if the objects themselves do not exist. For example, residents at pleasure centers could enjoy Flemish painting as an intentional object, even if the paintings themselves were not present.

Therefore, to save my position I need to show that there is an important difference between the "real" enjoyment of a higher pleasure and the enjoyment of a higher pleasure produced by artificial stimulation that

CRITIQUE OF QUANTITATIVE UTILITARIANISM

is not present in the comparison of the enjoyment of "real" and artificially induced lower pleasures. First, there does seem to be somewhat of a difference even in the case of the value of lower pleasures. For some reason I don´t fully comprehend, people are inclined to value the pleasure of eating a slice of watermelon over the pleasure gained from eating a stick of watermelon-flavored candy. But whatever evaluative gap is present between the real and artificial experience of the lower pleasures, I find that we are strongly inclined to find an immensely larger gap between the real and artificial experience of the higher pleasures. The difference in value between the pleasures of studying Plato and the artificial stimulation thereof seems immense. My critique of Quantitative Utilitarianism is weaker than I wish it were. I would like to show that the absurdity of establishing pleasure centers only counts against Quantitative Utilitarianism because the enjoyment of the higher pleasures is possible only by really studying Philosophy and really appreciating Art, but this is not so. Still, it is true that the lower pleasures lend themselves more easily to artificial stimulation, and thus, the establishment of pleasure centers is less likely under Qualitative Utilitarianism than under Quantitative Utilitarianism.

Therefore, the implications of both theories tend somewhat towards the Pleasure Center Interpretation. However, the implications of Qualitative Utilitarianism are much less inclined in that direction, and the life of the pleasure center residents as described under Qualitative Utilitarianism, although queer, is much less absurd than the life of those described under Quantitative Utilitarianism.

As for the Reduction Interpretation, it is clearly false. Even in the unlikely case in which the implications of both theories are that we ought to build pleasure centers, the lives of the residents therein would be quite different, and thus, the implications of one theory are not reduced to the implications of the other. Further, on the more likely assumption that the qualitative theory does not lead to the Pleasure Center Interpretation, the Reduction Interpretation is easily dismissed, for what could have greater fecundity and purity (given Quantitative Utilitarianism) than building pleasure centers? There are some adjustments that the Quantitative Utilitarian can make in ascribing a

CRITIQUE OF QUANTITATIVE UTILITARIANISM

higher value to what the Qualitative Utilitarian finds to be higher pleasures, but the fecundity and purity factors are insufficient to show that the practical implications of the two theories are similar. The practical implications of Quantitative Utilitarianism tend strongly to building pleasure centers where simple pleasure sensations are artificially stimulated. The practical implications of Qualitative Utilitarianism call for creating an environment in which as many people as possible enjoy those pleasures which are a part of lifestyles that have been found to be most desirable in the long run.

In "An outline of a system of utilitarian ethics", J.J.C. Smart explains and defends Quantitative Utilitarianism. He considers both the Pleasure Center and Reduction interpretations, but dismisses the former in favor of the latter. Since I am holding that the Pleasure Center Interpretation does describe the implications of Quantitative Utilitarianism, I must show that Smart is in error. Smart describes a situation similar to the Pleasure Center Interpretation, but finds it to be of no practical importance because it falls within the realm of "science fiction" and is a "remote possibility".(pp. 24-25) If the Pleasure Center Interpretation can be so easily dismissed then something more like the Reduction Interpretation must be correct, from which it follows that there is less of a difference between the practical implications of the two theories.

The Pleasure Center Interpretation is not science fiction in the sense that it is pure fantasy, which is the sense that Smart's position requires. The technology of artificial pleasure stimulation by electrical means is well established, and is likely to improve in the near future. The stimulation of pleasure by the use of drugs is well known and is currently a controversial social issue. The understanding of the political and social structures necessary to reform society into the mold of pleasure centers is within reach. There are science fiction stories, Brave New World for example, with themes similar to the Pleasure Center Interpretation, but the exploration of outer space is also a popular topic in science fiction and, yet, that is no reason for dismissing it as being philosophically unimportant.

CRITIQUE OF QUANTITATIVE UTILITARIANISM

The Pleasure Center Interpretation is not merely science fiction. It is a remote possibility, but that alone is insufficient to dismiss it as being unimportant. Only when the practical implications of a theory are a remote possibility for reasons independent of the theory are the practical implications unimportant. For example, it is a remote possibility that we will soon migrate to Venus even if we believed that we ought to on account of some ethical theory. The possibility of our doing so is remote because of technological limitations, a factor independent of the theory. It was also a remote possibility that the great cathedrals of Europe would have been built in the Middle Ages, except that people strongly believed that there existed a Supreme Being that desired to be so worshipped. Without the belief, and so, dependent on the theory, it was a remote possibility that they would be built, but once the theory was adopted, then it ceased to be a remote possibility. Building a system of pleasure centers is presently a remote possibility for reasons more like the case of the cathedrals than that of migrating to Venus. It is a remote possibility that pleasure centers will be built only on the assumption that those in power do not strongly believe in Quantitative Utilitarianism. If Quantitative Utilitarianism came to be held in the esteem that Christianity was held in the 15th century, then building pleasure centers would cease to be a remote possibility. Taken in themselves, pleasure centers are no more absurd than cathedrals from the perspective of someone who holds neither theory.

Thus, if building pleasure centers is the practical implication of Smart's theory, and if it is unlikely that they will be built for reasons dependent on the theory, then he and all others who share his view are saddled with the Pleasure Center Interpretation. Thus, the practical implications of Quantitative Utilitarianism are near the extreme described by the Pleasure Center Interpretation, and therefore, the Reduction Interpretation is false. The practical implications of the Pleasure Center Interpretation are absurd. And therefore, if there is a defensible version of utilitarianism, it is more likely to be based on Qualitative Hedonism than Quantitative Hedonism.

3. QUALITATIVE HEDONISM

The second chapter of Mill's <u>Utilitarianism</u> contains the classic statement of Qualitative Hedonism. So, I shall begin with Mill's definition (pp. 8-9), which goes as follows (with my added notation):

> If I am asked what I mean by difference of quality in pleasures, or what makes one pleasure more valuable than another, merely as a pleasure, [1] except it being greater in amount, there is but one possible answer. Of two pleasures, [2] if there be one to which all or almost all who have experience of both give a decided preference, [3] irrespective of any feeling of moral obligation to prefer it, that is the more desirable pleasure. If one of the two is, [4] by those who are competently acquainted with both, placed so far above the other that they prefer it, [5] even though knowing it to be attended with a greater amount of discontent, and [6] would not resign it for any quantity of the other pleasure which their nature is capable of, we are justified in ascribing to the preferred enjoyment [7] a superiority in quality so far outweighing quantity as to render it, in comparison, of small account.

This paragraph is a careful summary of several points that Mill develops in support of his position.

Point #1 is a clear statement that Mill's view is not Quantitative Hedonism.(25) A qualitative theory can admit some quantitative comparisons, but is not limited

---

25. Some argue that by `higher pleasure´, Mill simply means pleasures of a high intensity, which leads to interpreting Mill as a quantitative hedonist. There are passages in which Mill slips into speaking as if his view were quantitative hedonism and some

to them. By "quality" of pleasure, at this time, Mill seems to mean superiority in value apart from quantitative comparison, for he is allowing for pleasure of lesser quantity to have greater value. In the above quotation, Mill is clearly not saying that higher pleasures are merely more intense pleasures. If one holds (unlike Mill) that qualitative hedonism is inconsistent then this is a way to save Mill´s view, and this might be the motivation for interpreting him as being a quantitative hedonist.

Points #2, #4, #5, and #6 are a summation of Mill´s view on how we are to know which pleasures are superior. These topics will be further discussed in detail in the following section, titled "The Epistemology of Qualitative Hedonism". Mill does not say anywhere that the higher pleasures can be known by some intrinsic quality they all share. There is a tendency on the part of qualitative hedonists to identify the higher pleasures with those with a high degree of intellectual activity, but Mill never clearly commits himself to the view that intellectual activity is the mark of higher pleasures. Experience of the higher pleasures is the key to knowing that they are of superior value, but Mill does not say that our preference of them makes them higher pleasures. Instead, his view seems to be that there is no single intrinsic quality by which the higher pleasures can be known, and that is why experience of them is the only way that they can be identified. It is possible that something at one time is classified as a higher pleasure and with the further refinement of the judgment process the classification is overturned. Thus, the preference of competent judges does not make something a higher pleasure. Rather, their judgment is the best method by which the higher pleasures can be known.

The idea behind Point #3 is that, at the initial stages, our preconceptions of what pleasures are legitimate should be disregarded. The best possible evidence of the value of a type of pleasure is the testimony of

---

commentators have seized upon these passages in order to support a quantitative hedonist interpretation of Mill. See Gibbs´s "Higher and Lower Pleasures", pp. 33-34, and Sosa´s "Mill´s <u>Utilitarianism</u>", pp. 161-172.

those who have no strong preconceptions about the value of that type of pleasure before they have experienced it. Mill is saying in Point #7 that the difference in preference need not be absolute in order to justify making a qualitative distinction. He can still put a small value on the lower class of pleasures, but there is such a gap between them and the higher class that the distinction is well founded. Claiming that one class of pleasures is qualitatively superior does not imply that other classes are without value. The point is that no amount of the lower class is compensation for a life devoid of pleasures of the higher class. Assuming that sufficient higher pleasures are included in one's life, then there is value in the occasional experience of the lower pleasures. If experience of the higher pleasures is not possible, there is still some value in the experience of the lower pleasures. The key point of the distinction is that a life barely sufficient in the higher pleasures is more desirable than a life lacking them, but rich in the lower pleasures.

4. THE CHARGE OF INCONSISTENCY

Before I go any farther, I must answer the objection that all forms of Qualitative Hedonism are inconsistent, for there is little point in proceeding if this objection cannot be answered. From a philosophical point of view, this is a most serious objection, because to say that a theory is inconsistent amounts to saying that it cannot be true on logical grounds. An inconsistent theory is one based on contradictory hypotheses. The theory that the Earth was at the center of the solar system was based on the hypothesis that the Earth was created at the center of a perfect world designed to house God's favorite creatures. This hypothesis proved to be inconsistent with astronomical observations it was purported to explain. That a theory is inconsistent casts doubts on its application and support at all levels, for the inconsistency can affect any implication that is seen to follow from it. Once the Earth was shown not to be at the center of the universe, doubts arose concerning other implications of the hypothesis, for instance, that humans are creatures favored by the Creator of the universe.

G.E. Moore was not the first to claim that Qualitative Hedonism is inconsistent. Similar objections were raised by Henry Sidgwick in his <u>Methods of Ethics</u>

THE CHARGE OF INCONSISTENCY

(pp. 94-95) and F.H. Bradley in his Ethical Studies (pp. 116-120) thirty years prior to the publication of Principia Ethica in 1903. Since Moore devotes more space and detail to the problem, I shall concentrate on the arguments put forth in Principia Ethica.

The main point of the objection centers on the claim that hedonism identifies a single quality, pleasure, as being intrinsically valuable. It seems that if only one quality is valuable then, if one thing or state of affairs is more valuable than another, it must be so because there is a greater quantity of that single valuable quality in it. But, according to Qualitative Hedonism, the experience of a "higher" pleasure is more valuable than the experience of a "lower" pleasure, even if there is a smaller amount of pleasure present in the experience of the higher pleasure. The objectors conclude that the higher pleasure is held to be more valuable than the lower pleasure for some reason other than the pleasure present in it. And thus, what is claimed to be Qualitative Hedonism is not really hedonism, since it must import some criterion of value other than pleasure.

More precisely, my interpretation of Moore's argument is that to accept Qualitative Hedonism is to accept the following five propositions, which he goes on to claim are inconsistent:

1. Something is valuable [V] if and only if it is properly called a pleasure [P].

2. Something is properly called a `pleasure´ if and only if it has the quality "Q" unique and common to all pleasures.

3. One thing is more valuable than another [Vxy] if it has more of the quality [Qxy] unique and common to that which is the standard of value.

4. If one thing is more valuable than a second thing then the second thing is not more valuable than the first.

5. There are cases such that "l" is a pleasure and "h" is a pleasure and "l" has more of the quality unique and common to pleasures in it than "h", and yet,

THE CHARGE OF INCONSISTENCY

6. "h" is more valuable than "l".

The proof goes as follows, with lines one through six being a translation of the above six propositions:

1. $(x)(Vx > Px)$

2. $(x)(Px > Qx)$

3. $(x)(y)(Qxy > Vxy)$

4. $(x)(y)(Vxy > \sim Vyx)$

5. Qlh

6. Vhl

7. $Qlh > Vlh$ 3., Universal Instantiation.

8. Vlh 5. & 7., <u>modus ponens</u>.

9. $Vlh > \sim Vhl$ 4., Universal Instantiation.

10. $\sim Vhl$ 9. & 8., <u>modus ponens</u>.

11. $Vhl \ \& \sim Vhl$ 6. & 10., Conjunction.

Therefore, given this interpretation of Qualitative Hedonism, it is, indeed, an inconsistent position. From it follows that pleasure "h" is more valuable than pleasure "l" and pleasure "h" is not more valuable than pleasure "l", a contradiction. If there is an interpretation of Qualitative Hedonism that is consistent, and I think there is, then propositions 1. through 6. need to be amended so that the inconsistency is eliminated.

Proposition 1. seems correct, for the meaning of `Hedonism´ depends directly on the meaning of `pleasure´ and `value´. To claim `Hedonism´ is true simply is to claim that only `pleasure´ is `valuable´. It is like the meaning of `food´ is `nourishment´ for some `living thing´. If `nourishment´ meant something else than it does then `food´ might mean what we understand instead by `poison´. My point is a simple one. The meaning of some terms is more fundamental than the meaning of others, especially in cases in which a general concept is defined as some relation between two simpler concepts. There is no point in disputing what

THE CHARGE OF INCONSISTENCY

is meant by `Hedonism´, for the philosophical issues center on the meanings of `pleasure´ and `value´.

Propositions 2. and 3. come directly from Moore´s argument for the inconsistency of Qualitative Hedonism, for he writes in <u>Principia Ethica</u> (pp. 78-80):

> `Pleasant´ must, if words are to have any meaning at all, denote some one quality common to all the things that are pleasant; and, if so, then one can only be more pleasant than another, according as it has more or less of this one quality...

> ...if you say `pleasure,´ you must mean `pleasure´: you must mean some one thing common to all different `pleasures,´ some one thing, which may exist in different degrees, but which cannot differ in <u>kind</u>.

Notice that the first half of the first quotation is the second proposition of the preceding proof and the second quotation is the third proposition. Moore is claiming that the third proposition follows from the second.

In regard to the first of the two preceding quotations, Moore is saying that `pleasure´ singles out a class that includes all the things that are pleasures and nothing else. If there is such a class then there must be some formula that defines class membership within it. It is not necessary that the formula be unique, as Moore seems to be saying, for the description `the largest state in the U.S.A.´ denotes the same class as `the latest state to join the U.S.A.´. But, in the case of the set denoted by `pleasure´, it is a plausible assumption, for pleasures are a set with a wide and varied membership, so it would be a strange coincidence if two formulas denoted identical sets in a way that would mislead us.

At first sight, the point of the second of the two preceding quotations seems quite correct. For example, if it were true instead that only money is valuable, then $10 is obviously more valuable than $1. It is a case of "the more, the better". If pleasure sensations

THE CHARGE OF INCONSISTENCY

are homogeneous then it seems correct that more pleasure, meaning greater intensity and/or duration, is more valuable than less. The point of the objection to Qualitative Hedonism is that if a pleasure with less of the "Q" factor (a higher pleasure) is valued over a pleasure with more "Q" (a lower pleasure) then there must be some other factor than "Q" that explains the preference (I´ll call it "X"). "X" does not denote the class of pleasures, nor does it seem to denote some subset of the class in the relevant manner. Since "X" is a reason for one experience being more valuable than another, and since "X" is not pleasure, it is false that only pleasure is valuable and therefore, Qualitative Hedonism is not a legitimate variety of hedonism.

Moore draws an analogy between pleasure and color to illustrate the above point.(26) Suppose that `color´ denotes the class of things that are particular instances of all of the different shades of red, blue, yellow, <u>etc.</u>, and suppose that only color is valuable in the way that, according to hedonism, only pleasure is valuable. `More color´ means a brighter or deeper color as could be agreed upon by the comparison of color tiles in some way. To find a light blue to be more valuable than a dark green would roughly correspond to Qualitative Hedonism. Why is the light blue more valuable? It must be for some reason other than the color present, so to claim that light blue is more valuable than dark green is to claim that some other factor than color is valuable, and so, this is to abandon the initial assumption. But why not reply, it is still only color that is valuable, it is only that any shade of blue is intrinsically more valuable than any shade of green? This corresponds to the reply, "Yes, I still find that only `pleasures´ are valuable, it is just that I now find that some kinds of pleasures are more valuable than others." I think, as the argument stands, Moore is quite right, this is not really hedonism anymore. For example, if a hedonist values the pleasure of drinking organic carrot juice over the pleasure of drinking Kool-Aid, even though there is less pleasure in the former, then why is this so? If it is on account of a non-hedonistic factor, for example,

---

26. <u>Principia Ethica.</u>, pp. 80-81. Also see Cohen´s "J.S. Mill´s Qualitative Hedonism, pp. 155-156.

that organically-grown products have intrinsic value then in this respect, he is no longer a hedonist, but has shed that ideal in favor of some other.

In the context of the question at hand, Moore does not tell us exactly what the formula is that denotes `pleasure´, but earlier (p. 12) in Principia Ethica, he writes:

> Suppose a man says `I am pleased´ ...Well, if it is true, what does that mean? It means that his mind... has at this moment a certain definite feeling called pleasure.

Moore is here describing some variation of The Sensation Theory of Pleasure. So, Moore must mean the "Q" factor by which episodes are identified as being `pleasures´ to be the presence of a pleasurable sensation as a constituent of a mental event. And thus, his argument shows that Qualitative Hedonism is inconsistent only if the Sensation Theory of pleasure is assumed. The contradiction is derived from the assumption that pleasure is identified with a simple quality `Q´, and that an episode is more or less pleasant depending on the amount of `Q´ present in it. The Desire Theory of pleasure does not require a simple quality that identifies particular psychological episodes as being pleasures. There need not exist any simple quality that identifies all of the actual and possible objects of desire. In fact, the observations that almost anything can come to be desired by anyone and that exactly opposite things can be desired by different people seems to rule out that possibility.

The analysis of `pleasures´ within the Desire Theory of pleasure is similar to the analysis of `games´ that Wittgenstein gives in his Philosophical Investigations (pp. 31-32). There, he explains how the many different applications of a term like `game´ are connected by means of a "family resemblance". A theory like this holds that referring to something like Moore´s "Q" factor is not necessary in the legitimate use of a general term, if, as Moore says, "words are to have any meaning at all". Since the Desire Theory of pleasure doesn´t require something like Moore´s `Q´ factor, then the argument for the inconsistency of Qualitative Hedonism no longer holds, because the desirability of

THE CHARGE OF INCONSISTENCY

any given pleasure and the criterion by which a pleasure is identified no longer determined by a single, simple quality.

If this is all true, then the question arises, Why have so many highly respected philosophers been so wrong about such an important, but not especially difficult, issue? The consensus seems to be that any qualitative theory is inconsistent, but the preceding analysis shows that the inconsistency depends on accepting the Sensation Theory of pleasure, a theory that is in itself dubitable and a theory that Mill did not advocate. The list of philosophers who have held that Mill's doctrine is inconsistent includes Henry Sidgwick (1874), F.H. Bradley (1876), T.H. Green (1883), G.E. Moore (1903), W.D. Ross (1930), J.J.C. Smart (1961), Jan Narveson (1967), and Richard Brandt (1979), just to name a few. I do not pretend to fully understand the motivation of these fine thinkers on this point, but I think, to a significant degree, the answer to this question lies within a quote from Sidgwick's Methods of Ethics (pp. 120-121):

> But, as has been before said, in the common notions of `interest,´ `happiness,´ etc., there is a certain amount of vagueness and ambiguity so that in order to fit these terms for the purposes of scientific discussion, we must, while retaining the main part of their signification, endeavour to make it more precise. In my judgment this result is attained if by `greatest possible Happiness´ we understand the greatest attainable surplus of pleasure over pain; the two terms being used, with equally comprehensive meanings, to include respectively all kinds of agreeable and disagreeable feelings. Further, if this quantitative definition of the end be accepted, consistency requires that pleasures should be sought in proportion to their pleasantness; and therefore the less pleasant consciousness must not be preferred to the more pleasant, on the ground of any other qualities that it may possess. The distinctions of quality that Mill and others urge may still be admitted as grounds of preference, but only so far as they can be resolved into distinctions of quantity.

THE EPISTEMOLOGY OF QUALITATIVE HEDONISM

Some philosophers, like Bradley, Green, and Ross find all forms of hedonism lacking, so their objections go deeper than those of the above quote. But for the hedonists, I think it is that desire for precision and being "scientific" that has driven them to the side of Quantitative Hedonism. It is true that `pleasure´ and `happiness´ are difficult terms to precisely define. But in adopting definitions of pleasure and happiness based on the Sensation Theory of pleasure, philosophers have "thrown out the baby with the bathwater", meaning that there is a jewel of a theory, Qualitative Hedonism based upon the Desire Theory of Pleasure, that they have overlooked in their quest for philosophical precision. What value is there in increased precision, if it leads to the absurd practical implications of Quantitative Hedonism, and, ultimately, the demise of utilitarianism?

To sum up, what is now established at a very general level is that hedonism is defined by either the Sensation Theory of Pleasure or the Desire Theory of Pleasure, and that hedonism can take either the form of Quantitative Hedonism or Qualitative Hedonism. Quantitative Hedonism has absurd implications and Qualitative Hedonism is inconsistent, if we assume the Sensation Theory of pleasure. From this it follows that the only plausible form of hedonism that remains is Qualitative Hedonism as defined by some variation of the Desire Theory of pleasure. Qualitative Hedonism avoids the charge of inconsistency, and therefore, we may safely proceed in its formulation and defense.

5. THE EPISTEMOLOGY OF QUALITATIVE HEDONISM

The most pressing question in the epistemology of Qualitative Hedonism is, "How do we know that one pleasure is qualitatively superior in value to another?" Again, I begin by reference to the second chapter of <u>Utilitarianism</u>. Mill´s first argument originates in his response to the criticism that hedonism is a philosophy only fit for swine. To only seek pleasure, whether from the perspective of the individual or from the perspective of society, is often held to be a shallow view. We assume that humans have a nobler purpose in life than merely fulfilling desires for pleasures. Mill adroitly redirects the objection back to the critics of hedonism. To equate humans only seeking pleasure with swine only seeking pleasure

THE EPISTEMOLOGY OF QUALITATIVE HEDONISM

implies that humanity's capacity for pleasures is no different then that of swine. So it is the critics, not the hedonists, who depreciate humanity. Their objection to hedonism ignores the greater capacity humans have for the enjoyment of pleasure. This is ambiguous, for a greater capacity can mean either simply a capacity for more pleasure or it can mean a capacity for superior kinds of pleasure. If by greater capacity is meant the former, then this is no departure from Quantitative Hedonism. It is clear that Mill means the latter, for he writes:

> Human beings have faculties more elevated than animal appetites and, when once made conscious of them, do not regard anything as happiness which does not include their gratification.(Utilitarianism, p. 8)

Mill is here relying on the classical view, as put forth by Plato in the Republic (580d), that there are distinct kinds of pleasure that correspond to distinct kinds of mental faculties. It is also Plato's view that the pleasures of the reasoning faculty are superior to the pleasures of the spirited and appetitive faculties. (Republic 583a) Swine, presumably, lack the reasoning faculty, and so, are incapable of experiencing the pleasures related to it.

The above quotation also indicates that Mill has something other than the Sensation Theory of pleasure in mind when he is putting forth his views on the value of pleasure. He goes on to write in Utilitarianism (p. 8):

> ...there is no known Epicurean theory of life which does not assign to the pleasures of the intellect, of the feelings and imagination, and of the moral sentiments a much higher value as pleasures than to those of mere sensation...It is quite compatible with the principle of utility to recognize the fact that some kinds of pleasure are more desirable and more valuable than others.

The epistemological question that arises is, "How do we

know that pleasures are distinct by their being pleasures of distinct mental faculties?" I do not think that there has ever been a satisfactory answer given to this question. It is true that we can usually differentiate between the pleasures of studying Plato and eating a candy bar. But it is quite possible that the "mental" pleasure of studying Plato is really the mental activity of studying accompanied by a pleasure sensation. Supporting this is the observation that I find a very similar mental activity, the study of the works of Aristotle, not to be pleasurable. Further, sometimes it is pleasant to study Plato and at other times it is not, even if I am studying identical passages and thinking the same thoughts. This could be explained by my experiencing a pleasurable sensation one time and not the other.(27) On the other hand, I am quite sure that there are times when studying is a pleasant activity and yet no pleasure sensation occurs. Those who hold the Sensation Theory of pleasure must either claim that the activity really is not a pleasure, which is not a very plausible response, or that I am actually experiencing a pleasure sensation at the time but am unaware of it, an equally implausible response. I do not mean to rule out Mill's initial position. It is probably true that different kinds of beings have different capacities for pleasure. The problem is that without a sophisticated Phenomenology and Philosophy of Mind, which Mill had not developed, there is insufficient evidence on this point to justify a qualitative distinction in the value of pleasure.

Nevertheless, Mill doesn't need the "higher capacity" argument, because the following "trading places" and "competent judges" arguments, which I will come to shortly, are sufficient to make his case. Also, the "higher capacity" argument is not easily subsumed within Mill's empiricist epistemology, for what experience can we point to that clearly indicates that humans have a higher capacity for pleasure based on their elevated faculties?

----

27. This same kind of reasoning leads Gosling to a similar conclusion that "pleasure belongs to the class of things which are modifications of our awareness, like sensations and feelings" in Pleasure and Desire, pp. 28-29.

THE EPISTEMOLOGY OF QUALITATIVE HEDONISM

My view on the question of the relation of hedonistic ethics to the empiricist epistemological tradition is that Qualitative Hedonism is truer to the basic principles of empiricism than Quantitative Hedonism. No doubt, this is surprising, since Quantitative Hedonism is the variety of hedonism most often held by those philosophers like J.J.C. Smart and Jan Narveson, who, presumably, see themselves as being in the empiricist tradition. This is because Bentham´s hedonistic calculus, which is the foundation of all quantitatively-hedonistic views, is essentially rationalistic. What it seeks to determine is the value of various pleasurable psychological episodes. As I suppose is true with any hedonistic position, Benthamites require experience in order to quantify the intensity, duration, etc., of the pleasure, but absolutely no experience is necessary to make an evaluation of the pleasure once it has been quantified! In regard to this point, they have departed from their empiricist principles. They have a formula for evaluation which has no basis in (and which I find contrary to) our everyday experience. There are two separate questions before us, the amount of pleasure present in the experience and the value of the pleasure. It is an open question if the answer to one is independent of the other, and so, we must rely on experience. To conclude that value is totally dependent on amount is to apply only reason to the problem and to ignore the role of experience. If we forget the "higher capacity" argument, Mill´s theory is compatible with empiricism, for the "trading places" and "competent judges" arguments make no such commitment in the evaluation of pleasures independent of our experience of them.

G.E. Moore´s "Principle of Organic Unity" applies here, even though, oddly enough, Moore neglects to apply the principle to this problem. The Principle of Organic Unity is that the value of the whole is not necessarily the sum of the values of its parts. This definition of the Principle of Organic Unity is misleading, since it suggests that the whole/part relationship need be like the relationship between a house and its rooms, the parts being physically separable entities. Instead, the principle can be interpreted as saying that the value of the whole is not necessarily the sum of the values of each of its properties taken separately.(28) This is especially true if one holds the "bundle theory", that a particular thing is no more or less than the collection of its properties. The intensity, duration, and effect of a pleasant psychological episode are properties of the episode and so, can be interpreted as being its parts. Thus, a quantitative theory is a theory of valuation that computes the value of the whole as being the sum of the values of its parts. Therefore, quantitative theories of value are inconsistent with the Principle of Organic Unity, and thus, Moore's position, including his objections to qualitative hedonism is inconsistent.(29) Moore's position on this question is also a departure from the spirit of <u>Principia Ethica</u>. I understand the mainstay of his theory to be that "The Good" and our consciousness of "The Good" (our evaluative consciousness) to be a matter entirely separate from Nature and our way of thinking about Nature. That is why it is always an "open question" whether or not any property or entity in Nature is good.(30)

Benthamites are using a calculus (simple arithmetic) only known to be reliable in its application to natural objects in their evaluation of psychological episodes. They are no longer maintaining the natural/non-natural distinction, because they are assuming that the logic of "what is" is parallel to the logic of "what ought to be". The value of electricity (and other natural things) is the product of the intensity (watts) and the duration. We are billed for consuming so many kilowatt hours. But, according to the Principle of Organic Unity, the same logic need not apply to the evaluation of pleasure.

----

28. Moore's example of the relation of the parts of the body to the body itself suggests the opposite view (<u>Principia Ethica</u>, pp. 27-32), but the discussion that follows (pp. 37-41) upholds my interpretation. Also see Butchvarov's "That Simple, Indefinable, Non-natural Property <u>Good</u>", pp. 59-60.

29. Moore anticipates this objection in <u>Ethics</u>, pp. 105-107, but discusses it in the light of the quantity of pleasure as opposed to other factors like virtue, wisdom, and so forth, which is not helpful in the present case.

30. <u>Principia Ethica</u>, pp. 37-38.

THE EPISTEMOLOGY OF QUALITATIVE HEDONISM

Mill's "trading places" argument is based on a thought-experiment that goes as follows:

> Few human creatures would consent to be changed into any of the lower animals for a promise of the fullest allowance of a beast's pleasures; no intelligent human being would consent to be a fool, no instructed person would be an ignoramus, no person of feeling and conscience would be selfish and base, even though they would be persuaded that the fool, the dunce, or the rascal is better satisfied with his lot than they are with theirs.(Utilitarianism, p.9)

The argument, I am sure, is inspired by Plato's Philebus 21c-d. There, Socrates is comparing the value of pleasure to the value of intelligence. His interlocutor, Protarchus, finds himself speechless when he realizes that a life of total pleasure without intelligence "would be living the life not of a human being but of some sort of sea lung" (31), presumably, not a very desirable alternative. The argument is based on a thought-experiment. Assuming that you are a normal human being, would you exchange places with another being who, although incapable of enjoying the higher pleasures, enjoys the greatest possible quantity of pleasure? (At this point `quantity of pleasure´ means pleasure as defined by the Sensation Theory of Pleasure, and as calculated by Bentham's calculus.)

The argument is based upon experience, since we rely on our personal experience of the enjoyment of higher pleasures in making our judgment. This experience is compared to what you imagine life to be like without the higher pleasures but with the constant enjoyment of pleasurable sensations. It is true, but irrelevant, that most people are generally disinclined to trade places with anyone or anything. We fear the unknown and the chance of losing our identity, but

---

31. For further information on the connection between Mill and Plato, see Gibbs´ "Higher and Lower Pleasures", pp. 32-41.

these fears have nothing to do with what is at stake here. The thought-experiment can actually be more clearly framed if you imagine alternative futures for yourself without trading places with anyone or anything. The element of possibly losing your personal identity adds a dramatic, but misleading effect to the argument. I think that everyone in their right mind would choose not to trade away their present life for a life of the experience of continuous, intense sensations of pleasure. If a Quantitative Hedonist declines to trade places then he contradicts himself, since he is holding that a life of less pleasure is more valuable than a life of more pleasure.

The best argument for Qualitative Hedonism is what I am calling the "competent judges" argument. This is the argument that Mill gives when he writes:

> From this verdict of the only competent judges, [1] I apprehend there can be no appeal. On a question which is the best worth having of two pleasures, or [2] which of two modes of existence is [3] the most grateful to the feelings, [4] apart from its moral attributes and [5] from its consequences, the judgment of these who are qualified by knowledge of both, or, [6] if they differ, that of the majority of them, must be admitted as final.(Utilitarianism, p. 11)

Point #1 is that there can be no appeal to anything other than the findings of competent judges, that is, there is no more valid source of opinion than their experience, other sources being, I suppose, rationalistic theories, religious doctrines, cultural traditions, and the like. A competent judge need not be specially trained to make such a decision, and instead, is simply an ordinary citizen who would qualify as a juror in a court of law, that is, someone with a good mind and a basic education who is capable of making sound judgments on other questions. A special qualification would be that the judge have personal experience of the pleasures to be evaluated. The "evidence" cannot be supplied to the "court" in the form of briefs and lawyer´s appeals. The personal experience of a pleasure and the testimony of those who have experienced similar pleasures is the only way that one can become acquainted with the nature of a particular pleasure or kind of pleasure. Thus, the competent judges argument is based on principles compatible with empiricism. The argument is not circular, since the qualifications for being a competent judge are not the same as those of being a judge who by definition would choose what Mill finds to be the higher pleasures.(32)

This argument is also inspired by Plato. In the <u>Republic</u> 582a the pleasures of a philosopher ("the lover of wisdom") are compared to the pleasures of "the lover of victory" and "the lover of gain". Of course, if you ask them, each of these three types of personalities will probably recommend their own kind of pleasure. They are each in their own category just for that reason. So, whom are we to believe? Plato tells us, the philosopher is the best judge, for good judgment requires "experience, knowledge, and discussion..." qualities that the others lack. The philosopher has had some experience of the other two kinds of pleasure in the course of his life, but the others have not tasted the philosopher's fruit. The old man (Cephalus) at the opening scene of the <u>Republic</u> (328c-329e) was a person who had such a broad range of experiences, although he was not a philosopher in the narrow sense. Being moderately wealthy, he was able to experience the pleasures of monetary gain and the sensual pleasures that money can buy. Looking back on his life, he values most the companionship of learned friends in pursuit of a just life. The philosopher, and those who have had similar experiences, are the most knowledgeable of the three types of persons, and discussion is their specialty. On all three counts it is rational to follow their recommendation that the pleasures of the contemplative life are superior.

Point #2 concerns an important issue that will receive detailed consideration in the section titled "Pleasure and Happiness". There is a whole range of

---

32. According to Cohen, Mill is not <u>defining</u> a higher pleasure as one that is prefered by competent judges. Rather, their preference is a "criterion" of something being a higher pleasure. See "J.S. Mill's Qualitative Hedonism", p. 152.

pleasures that are open to our inspection and evaluation. There are particular pleasures, that is, the actual pleasurable episodes that occur in individuals. There are kinds of pleasures at every level of generality, ranging from the pleasures of drinking a specific brand of vodka by a specific type of individual in a specific type of situation, to the most general kind of category, as Mill puts it, "modes of existence" (<u>Utilitarianism</u>, p. 11) which I understand to be different lifestyles based upon the enjoyment of different types of pleasures, for example, the lifestyle of a classical musician living in New York City. It is not necessary to judge each particular pleasure separately because it is reasonable to suppose that similar pleasures will generally receive similar evaluations. If the study of the history of England is found to be highly enjoyable then it is likely that the study of the history of America will also prove to be enjoyable.

Point #3 is stated by Mill in a misleading way. When deciding which pleasures are superior, the judges are not deciding which are "the most grateful to the feelings", for putting it that way suggests the Sensation Theory of Pleasure and the Quantitative Hedonism that follows.(33) The judges are deciding which pleasures are most desirable, in the sense of which pleasures they would want most to be a part of their life. At this point, the pleasures are evaluated apart from their causal properties, for Point #5, the consequences of the pleasure, handles that. What Mill has in mind is a tribunal put together in order to evaluate pleasures in the most unbiased manner possible. The evaluation of pleasures is to be of the pleasures, taken in themselves, apart from their consequences and any prejudices that the judges may have about them.

----

33. Mill is not very careful in his use of the term, `pleasure´. Sometimes, he means by it pleasure sensations (or "feelings"), which I understand <u>not</u> to be what he ultimately means by `pleasure´. This leads Edwards to interpret (incorrectly, I think) Mill as holding the Heterogeneous Sensation Theory of pleasure in <u>Pleasures and Pains</u>, pp 32-34.

THE EPISTEMOLOGY OF QUALITATIVE HEDONISM

Point #4 is crucial, although no explanation of it is given by Mill. The judges are asked to evaluate a pleasure "apart from its moral attributes", which is misleading, since their judgment is the way, within this theory, that pleasures are evaluated for their ethical worthiness. What Mill means is that the when judges are evaluating pleasures they are to temporarily put aside whatever moral prejudices they might have in regard to them. This is the point where the argument no longer can be an appeal to an actual tribunal, and so, is the point of departure for philosophical speculation. We cannot test the theory by putting together an actual tribunal because no one is free from prejudice in this area. Juries taken from different times and places will give very different evaluations of pleasures. Most people are incapable of making unprejudiced evaluations in this area because a great part of their cultural backgrounds is based upon the sanction and prohibition of certain types of pleasurable activities, and these prejudices are deeply imbedded. A jury of traditional Christians is likely to place a high value on Bible study and a low value on "exploring one's sexuality". A different jury will arrive at very different values. Mill's solution, point #6, is that if the judges differ then the decision of the majority is taken. At best, this is imprecise. If an overwhelming percentage of competent judges deem a pleasure to be of extraordinary quality, I might be satisfied, but if only 51% did then I would not be satisfied. It is safe to assume that no one is immune to variations in attitudes about different kinds of pleasures that have their basis in prejudices fostered in their upbringing. Thus, it really isn't possible to have a jury that consists of actual citizens acting as competent judges in regard to the issues at hand.

Therefore, as often happens in Philosophy, we must rely upon our powers of imagination and speculation. I am not saying that this means that conclusions based upon imagination and speculation are unreliable. I place great (but not unquestioning) value on the views of those acknowledged to be the great thinkers of history and of the present time. Mill seems to hold that the enjoyment of the intellectual pleasures is of the highest value, and this generally corresponds to the views of the great thinkers.

THE EPISTEMOLOGY OF QUALITATIVE HEDONISM

Also very helpful in determining what is the good life are individuals who, for one reason or the other, are unrestrained by social pressures and experiment with lifestyles and pleasures generally unapproved by society. These rebels range from characters like Oscar Wilde, Edgar Allen Poe, the "hippies" of the 1960s, "liberals" (including John Stuart Mill), to Joseph Smith and Chairman Mao. We have learned from both the successes and failures of these people. Often, the true test of the validity of their views lies in the formation of a society based upon their beliefs. I doubt if a society based on complete anarchy would prosper, and societies such as that of the nineteenth century Mormons, with an excess of prohibitions, are too rigid.

Mill's use of competent judges is analogous to John Rawls' use of persons in the "original position" in his A Theory of Justice (p. 21). Rawls puts a loaded question to his judges when they are asked to agree upon "certain principles of justice", for this assumes that the type of question to ask is one of rules. Mill asks his judges, what is the good life?, and then proceeds to devise a theory in which as many people as possible are given the opportunity to live it. Presumably, the implications of Mill's theory will be derived with this end in mind. Why don't those judges in Rawls's "original position" concur with Mill, and find the "principles of justice" to be parallel to those prescribed by qualitative hedonism? The difference in the findings of the two hypothetical panels is that Rawl's panel puts individual rights of liberty and rights of each individual to benefit from public policy ahead of utility, and Mill's panel puts utility ahead of individual rights. In support of his position, Rawls brings in the idea of risk. We are to imagine the absurdity of a slaveholder explaining to his slaves that in the original position it was found that maximizing average utility would be achieved by allowing people to sell themselves and their descendants into slavery, and through a series of bargains over the years, he happens to be an owner and they happen to be slaves (pp. 167-169). The point is that liberty is so precious that it alone cannot be bargained away in the original position. I am holding that Mill's competent judges would place a high, though not absolute, value on personal liberty, since it is an important part of the good life.

PLURALISTIC QUALITATIVE HEDONISM

For practical reasons, there will be as much liberty in a society based on consequentialism as one based upon rights. I overheard the following remark at a convention: "I was once a utilitarian, but when all the problems of justice and distribution came up, I switched to Rights Theory". The problems of utilitarianism (some of which this essay solves) are dwarfed by the problems inherent in Rights Theory. Due to the complexity of the world, it is impossible to protect the rights of every actual and potential person, and there really is no way to arbitrate all of these conflicting claims to rights. From utilitarianism, as herein conceived, follow plenty of rights, and a method of arbitrating conflicting claims. Instead of the trouble to establish massive court systems, overly intricate laws, and a legion of attorneys to advocate each individual´s claims to rights, if we instead simply tried to maximize overall benefits in an enlightened and efficient manner, the end result would be more people enjoying greater freedom. If it were really possible to guarantee everyone´s rights then adopting utilitarianism as a "principle" would involve risking the liberty of people outside the original position without their consent. But since it is not possible to guarantee their liberty under any system, then there really is no such "risk" taken.

6. PLURALISTIC QUALITATIVE HEDONISM

I began the chapter by giving a negative definition of Qualitative Hedonism as being hedonism that is not quantitative. Since Qualitative Hedonism is defined negatively, it is open to a wide range of variations, while there is a limited range within Quantitative Hedonism. The variety of Qualitative Hedonism that has received by far the most attention is the view I am calling `Dualistic Qualitative Hedonism´. According to this theory, there are two classes of pleasures, the higher pleasures and the lower pleasures. The distinction between higher and lower pleasures follows the classic dualistic distinction between mind and body. The higher pleasures are associated with intellectual activities, studying Philosophy and the appreciation of Fine Arts, for example, and the lower pleasures are associated with bodily activities, prime examples being the pleasures of eating and sexual activity. Although he is not very clear on this point, Mill can be interpreted as being a Dualistic Qualitative Hedonist.

PLURALISTIC QUALITATIVE HEDONISM

It is the pleasures of Socrates, someone known to be absorbed in intellectual pursuits, that are compared to the pleasures of the pig. Examples Mill gives of higher pleasures necessary for human happiness are:

> ...interest...in the objects of nature, the achievements of art, the imaginations of poetry, the incidents of history, the ways of mankind, past and present, and their prospects in the future.(Utilitarianism, p. 14)

and these all seem to be of the intellectual class.

A theory of value that has (to my knowledge) never been given serious and detailed philosophical consideration is a variety of Qualitative Hedonism different from the standard Dualistic Qualitative Hedonism. I will call it `Pluralistic Qualitative Hedonism´.(34) According to it, pleasures do not cleanly fit into the two categories, intellectual and bodily, and more important, the value of pleasures does not exactly follow the intellect/body distinction. The qualitative differences of value that follow from Pluralistic Qualitative Hedonism are more complex than the parallel distinctions that follow from the dualistic theory.

Dualistic Qualitative Hedonism places such a great value on the higher pleasures that they are almost held to be incommensurable with the lower pleasures. This incommensurabilty is not absolute, as there are allowances for the values of the lower class. Mill puts it as follows:

> If one of the two is...placed so far above the other that they...would not resign it for any quantity of the other ...we are justified in ascribing to the preferred enjoyment a superiority in quality so far outweighing quantity as to render it, in comparison, of small account.(Utilitarianism, pp. 8-9)

----

34. Edwards discusses the distinction between qualitative hedonism and ethical pluralism in Pleasures and Pains, pp. 97-111.

PLURALISTIC QUALITATIVE HEDONISM

Thus, Mill's position is that the comparison of value of the two classes of pleasure is so different that we are justified in drawing a qualitative distinction between their respective values. Although valuable, no amount of the lower pleasures is compensation for a life devoid of sufficient higher pleasures. It is similar to comparing the values of coal and diamonds. It might seem that their values are commensurable, since coal is worth about one hundred dollars per ton and diamonds are worth about one thousand dollars per carat. They both have value measured in dollars based upon weight, but the difference is so great that, practically speaking, they are incommensurable in value. Coal is in the class of common raw materials. Diamonds are in the class of precious jewels. A life without diamonds is bearable, as there is a sufficient number of other beautiful things in the world to appreciate. A life without sufficient higher pleasures is unbearable, and no amount of the pleasures of eating, drinking, sunbathing, and so forth, would compensate for this loss. Mill writes:

> It is better to be a human being dissatisfied than a pig satisfied; better to be Socrates dissatisfied than a fool satisfied. And if the fool, or the pig, are of a different opinion, it is because they only know their side of the question. The other party to the comparison knows both sides.(<u>Utilitarianism</u>, p. 10)

The key point in Mill's view is that no amount of the lower pleasures are compensation for a life devoid of the higher pleasures. There is still value placed upon them, but that value cannot accumulate to the point of being compensation for not having any of the higher pleasures. So, it is possible that, in some situations, the value of the pleasure of eating two candy bars is equivalent to the pleasure of studying Plato for one hour. The point is that a significant part of one's lifetime must be reserved for the enjoyment of the higher pleasures. After that, the values of two classes become commensurable. Of course, if the choice is between living and dying then the question of the quality of life doesn't come to bear. The avoidance of the pains of starvation and the lack of shelter are paramount. According to Dualistic Qualitative Hedonism, the enjoyment of the higher pleasures is necessary for the "good life".

My view is that the distinction between higher and lower pleasures does not exactly follow the distinction between mind and body that we think of as being the basis of the distinction between mental and bodily pleasures. I do place a great value on an intellectually active life, but I do not believe that all intellectual pleasures are superior to all pleasures that do not especially involve the intellect. For example, the pleasures of having, loving, and playing with children is a pleasure that I (and I imagine the competent judges) value highly. Having children (or some similar experience) may be necessary for the good life. These are pleasures that do not especially require or involve the intellect. People often become obsessed with intellectual activities to the point of detriment to themselves and others. Even the study of philosophy can be overdone to the point of one's being so obsessed with one's specialty that the pleasures taken in it come to have little value. People often take great pleasure in plotting the demise of others, an intellectual pleasure of little redeeming value. So, clearly, simply because a pleasure involves intellectual activity does not make it valuable, and there are some pleasures that do not especially involve the intellect that do deserve being included in the higher category.

I conclude that there really are not two neat classes into which all pleasurable experiences fall, hence the title `Pluralistic Qualitative Hedonism'. In regard to value, there are higher pleasures, lower pleasures, and a whole range in between. Also, there appears to be no simple factor that explains how all of these different pleasures are to be ranked, which partially explains the need to appeal to the experience of competent judges.

In <u>Pleasures and Pains</u> (pp. 35-45), the only full-length work on the topic of qualitative hedonism, Rem Edwards proposes that the distinction between local and non-local pleasures offers prospects for explaining the qualitative difference in value between pleasures. The distinction itself seems valid. As opposed to Ryle's view that it only makes sense to ascribe location to pains Edwards holds a view developed by John Hospers that some pleasures (Freud's pleasures of the erogenous zones are an example) are experienced as having a location.(35) It is true that this distinction does roughly follow Mill's distinction between the higher and lower pleasures, and, I find, the same reasons that count against Dualistic Qualitative Hedonism also count against the localized/non-localized distinction. Some pleasures that I imagine that competent judges find to be of great value fall under each category, and likewise, so do pleasures of little value.

7. PLEASURE AND HAPPINESS

An explanation of Mill's views on the relation between pleasure and happiness (which generally coincide with my own) will clear up several yet unresolved questions. He holds the "theory of utility" which is also the "greatest happiness principle" and writes:

> Those who know anything about the matter are aware that every writer, from Epicurus to Bentham, who maintained the theory of utility meant by it, not something to be contradistinguished from pleasure, but pleasure itself, together with exemption from pain.(<u>Utilitarianism</u>, p. 6)

Mill means by happiness not being "contradistinguished" from pleasure that the two terms are interdefined. `Happiness´ is a life that contains `pleasure´ (with the proper balance of tranquility). The greatest `pleasure´ is that which is most `desirable´, which is one's own `happiness´, or taken from a larger perspective, `the greatest happiness for the greatest number´. Some forms of utilitarianism do not so interdefine pleasure and happiness and so are able to

---

35. See Gilbert Ryle's <u>Dilemmas</u>, pp. 57-58 and John Hospers' <u>Human Conduct</u>, p. 58. Susan Feagin is also critical of Edwards' suggestion that the local/non-local distinction will be of use in clarifying Qualitative Hedonism in her "Mill and Edwards on the Higher Pleasures", pp. 244-248.

PLEASURE AND HAPPINESS

make a distinction between maximizing pleasure (hedonistic utilitarianism) and maximizing happiness (eudaemonistic utilitarianism). Since the terms are interdefined in Mill's theory, his theory is equally hedonistic and eudaemonistic.

As for the exact relationship between pleasure and happiness, I think Mill's position is very well taken. `Happiness` is a life with the proper type, variety, and amount of `pleasure`. He writes:

> If by [1] happiness be meant a continuity of highly pleasurable excitement, [2] it is evident enough that this is impossible. [3] A state of exalted pleasure lasts only moments or in some cases, and with some intermissions, hours or days, and is the occasional brilliant flash of enjoyment, not its permanent and steady flame. Of this the philosophers who have taught that happiness is the end of life were as fully aware as those who taunt them. [4] The happiness which they meant was not a life of rapture, but moments of such, in an existence made up of few and transitory pains, many and various pleasures, with a decided prominance of the active over the passive, and having as the foundation of the whole not to expect more from life than it is capable of bestowing. (<u>Utilitarianism</u>, pp. 12-13)

Point #1 refers to the definition of happiness that follows from quantitative hedonism. If merely maximizing the enjoyment of pleasurable sensations is the end of life then happiness must (ideally) consist in the continuous enjoyment of pleasurable sensations. In point #2, Mill contends that this is impossible. He has not anticipated the development of artificial pleasure stimulation. Mill's argument against quantitative hedonism is not as powerful, for it begins with the premise that it is practically impossible for humans to continually enjoy pleasure. Recent technological advances indicate that continual enjoyment of pleasure is possible (See pp. 74-80.) The third point is based upon Mill's phenomenology of pleasure. He observes that the enjoyment of pleasure is only a fleeting, momentary experience. He is here reverting to the Sensation Theory of Pleasure, for a phenomenology of pleasure as defined within the Desire Theory is not so limited. The fulfillment of desires can be continual. For example, someone who has long desired to return to school and study Philosophy can be continually pleased at his or her doing so.

Mill's description of the happy life is like that of a gourmet of pleasures, carefully sampling pleasures and allowing ample time to "clear the palate" so to best enjoy the next one. Experiencing too much pleasure or experiencing too many pleasures of low quality, or not experiencing a sufficient variety of pleasures, all detract from the ideal happy life. I imagine that this is exactly the life that our hypothetical panel of competent judges would recommend.

It may be true that, taken in themselves, intense pleasurable sensations are most desirable, as seen from a limited perspective. But the fallacy of composition applies here because, taken as a whole, that is, as a way of life, this is no longer the most desirable alternative. What is desirable as a way of life supersedes what seems to be desirable at any given moment. It is consistent for a hedonist, as defined by the Desire Theory, to hold that the greatest pleasure, and the most desirable thing, is a happy life.

The preceding remarks are far from being a complete account of Qualitative Hedonism. As I have presented it, Qualitative Hedonism is a view based upon experience and observation. Through the ages, philosophers have addressed the question, "What kind of life is most worth living?", and, I suppose, their conclusions were based upon personal insights and observation of others. Providing an answer to this question could be furthered through sophisticated research in psychology and sociology. Broadly based studies of different lifestyles and their social effects are needed in order to make progress in this area.

CHAPTER FOUR

QUALITATIVE UTILITARIANISM

1. THE DEFINITION OF THE THEORY

As a general ethical theory, Qualitative Utilitarianism has already been defined as the theory that actions are right or wrong on account of the pleasure and pain that they produce as their consequences, and that the evaluation of pleasure and pain is a complex matter, not merely the quantification of a single quality. Different versions of Qualitative Utilitarianism that can be generated, depending on one´s theory of action and how pleasures are assessed. Specifically, the theory I am defending involves a careful combination of the features of General Consequentialism, as developed in Chapter One, and the features of Qualitative Hedonism, as developed in Chapter Three. In this final chapter, by `Qualitative Utilitarianism´ I mean the specific version of the theory that follows from the incorporation of the main points of the preceding chapters.

The main point of Chapter One is the clarification of an ambiguity inherent in the definition of consequentialism. I argue that the usual definition of consequentialism, that an action is right if and only if it has the best overall effects, does not prescribe a single course of action, and thus is inadequate as a decision procedure. The basis of the ambiguity is that there rarely is such a thing as an identifiable, singular set of consequences that can be attributed to a particular action. Each action occurs in a setting in which its outcome can vary according to subsequent actions and choices. Because future choices are still open, it is not possible to identify the optimific action as commonly understood within consquentialistic theories. The only coherent form of consequentialism as a decision procedure is one that is noncommital in regard to particular, isolated cases, and instead, prescribes a broad range of actions to be undertaken by the community at large.

There are two sides to a consequentialistic analysis of the ethical value of actions. The first is to provide a method by which past actions can be evaluated, and the second is to provide a theory by which we may choose the actions that will lead to the realization of our goals for the future. Since the past

THE DEFINITION OF THE THEORY

is settled, the complications introduced by the existence of divergent future choices and the complexities of group action mostly apply to the second future-oriented side of consequentialism. Clearly, it is the future-oriented side that is most important, as the main value in making ethical judgments of past actions lies in the lessons we can learn from them, and it is here that General Consequentialism best provides a coherent guide for our actions.

General Consequentialism describes an ideal set of consequences that is equivalent to the best possible outcome of the actions of everyone taken together. It also assigns responsibility to both groups and individuals for whatever difference occurs between the ideal outcome and the actual effects of actions. General Consequentialism has a very strong orientation towards results, with little allowance for excuses. It sets before the group or the individual that which ideally could have happened in comparison to what actually happened, and immediately the question, Why not the ideal?, is suggested.

General Consequentialism is a harsh doctrine. I don't believe any society or individual has or ever will attain perfection as so defined, or, in other words, no one will ever be able to continually perform the right action. An analysis of `right´ as referring to only one action in relation to all of its alternatives, which are `wrong´, only follows from theoretical assumptions quite different from those of utilitarians. If an action is `right´ only if it is performed for the correct reason, say, one's duty as seen to follow from the Categorical Imperative, then all other alternatives are clearly opposite and `wrong´. Because consequentialism looks at a myriad of possible outcomes, many of which are quite similar, it would be better to say that actions are more or less `right´ in proportion to the beneficial effects they produce. The right action is the one (if there is one above the others) that produces the greatest benefit, but other actions with benefits that approximate the action that is most beneficial are still properly `right´, to a degree.

So, if something must be done to properly identify those sets of consequences that are near those identified by the theory as being those of the `right´ action then this can be accomplished by the introduction of the notion of a "satisfactory" overall outcome. In other words, it is not the case that all outcomes other than the ideal outcome are equally wrong. There is a continuum, ranging from the worst to those approaching the best to, finally, the ideal outcome. If the outcome of an action approaches the ideal then it would be misleading to say, "It is wrong." "Satisfactory" is a better term for such instances.

Chapter Two is a discussion of hedonism, providing a background for the quantitative/qualitative distinction in Chapter Three. The main conclusion is that those things that are ultimately at the basis of ethical obligation are pleasures, as therein defined. What makes the doctrine in Chapter Three distinctive is its discriminations of value within the class of pleasures. In agreement with Mill, the importance of experience of a variety of pleasures is emphasized therein. The broader question within hedonism, concerning the relation of pleasure to happiness, is also discussed, and again, is presented as being in general agreement with Mill. Happiness is a life of tranquility, with a lack of pain and suffering, with the occasional well placed, high quality pleasurable experience.

2. THE PROOF OF THE THEORY

In this essay, consideration has already been given to the proof of Qualitative Utilitarianism. I have given arguments and observations in support of consequentialism, hedonism, and the superiority of the higher pleasures. This section will deal specifically with Mill's proof given in Chapter Four of <u>Utilitarianism</u>, as an analysis of it pertains to the proof of the theory as given in this essay. Also, I will discuss reactions to Mill's proof by philosophers in the 125 years since its initial publication.

"Of What Sort of Proof the Principle of Utility is Susceptible" is the awkward title of the fourth chapter of Mill's <u>Utilitarianism</u>. One might assume that Mill would provide a straightforward answer to the question posed by the title, but no. Most of the chapter is devoted to the proof itself, with only a few, scattered passages devoted to the topic of what sort of proof it is. A clear answer to the question would include setting out the different kinds of proof, and then, demonstrating that the proof of the Principle of

Utility is one kind of proof to the exclusion of the others, and that is how I will proceed.

It is an earlier work, A System of Logic (pp. 111-114), to which we must refer in order to find a detailed explanation of what Mill means by "proof". There he explains that a proof is given for a statement if we believe it to be true on the basis of some other statement from which it follows. Mill says that to infer from one statement to another is to give "credence" to the concluding statement. It is well known that Mill did extensive work in inductive logic. It is clear that Mill allows for both inductive and deductive proofs; the latter he calls "ratiocination". A deductive proof of a statement provides indubitable evidence for the truth of the conclusion, assuming the premises to be true, while an inductive proof provides evidence by which it is rational to believe the conclusion, but lacks the indubitability of deductive proofs. A further distinction needs to be drawn between statements that are at the foundation of a system of beliefs, and statements that are known on the basis of others, statements that must eventually be based upon statements that are at the foundation. It is an important aspect of Mill's theory that the Principle of Utility is the statement that lies at the foundation of his ethical theory. The status of the Principle of Utility within Mill's ethics is similar to the status of the Axiom of Uniformity (the future will resemble the past) within his theory of induction.(36) There is no deductive proof for this principle, for it is possible (although highly unlikely) that tomorrow we will find ourselves in a world that is radically different, where water runs uphill, snow is hot, and the sun rises in the West. In every new day we observe that the world has changed little. It might appear after the first snowstorm of winter that outside is a new world, but we know that similar snowstorms have occurred for thousands of Decembers past.

On Mill's view, all other knowledge based upon induction presupposes the Axiom of Uniformity, that the future will resemble the past. That every action will

---

36. Utilitarianism: with Critical Essays, pp. 7-9 (An excerpt from a later edition of A System of Logic).

THE PROOF OF THE THEORY

produce an equal reaction, that the force of gravity between two objects decreases proportionally to the square of the distance between them, that the fittest will survive, all presuppose that the future shall resemble the past. That is, each of these laws are hypothetical. It is only if the future will resemble the past that every action will produce an equal reaction, and so forth. Thus, the statement that lies at the foundation of science is this general hypothesis.

But, what is so special about this proposition, `the future will resemble the past´? Why is this proposition at the foundation of inductive science? The answer lies in the pragmatics of knowledge. Knowledge based on induction is knowledge that is based on past observations. We want to be effective. The success of employing inductive knowledge depends on the future resembling the past, for if there were no such resemblance, then the observations of the past would no longer serve as a reliable guide to the future. Knowledge based on induction has generally proven to be effective. Current technology is, to a great degree, based upon inductive knowledge, and it is effective in building roads, organizing data, and growing wheat. It is by this success that the Axiom of Uniformity is justified.

It is difficult to supply a hypothesis that might serve as an alternative to the Axiom of Uniformity. Its antithesis is that the future will not resemble the past. A world view based upon one interpretation of the Christian Faith contains an amendment to the Axiom of Uniformity, as it predicts a very different world order will inevitably come in the near future. Any prediction that future events will occur contrary to the principles of the past is opposed by the Axiom of Uniformity. Throughout history, people have predicted that things would soon become very different, but there has not yet been any drastic change, and so the Axiom of Uniformity has been constantly reconfirmed.

Thus, there is a hierarchy within inductive science that is neither based upon a most certainly known statement nor is the Axiom of Uniformity known chronologically prior to all others, nor is it based upon statements that are most obviously known through the senses. Instead, it is a hypothesis that is constantly being confirmed by our observation. The Axiom of

THE PROOF OF THE THEORY

Uniformity is at the foundations because of its relation to other statements that can be known by induction, the relation being that it alone is presupposed by all other claims to knowledge based upon induction.

The status of the Principle of Utility within Mill's ethics can be understood by comparing it to the status of the Axiom of Uniformity within his analysis of inductive science. The Principle of Utility is at the foundation of ethics, because, within this view, it is presupposed by all other ethical judgments. That the right action is the one that produces the greatest happiness for the greatest number presupposes the Principle of Utility. For this reason, there is no final proof of the Principle of Utility by reference to other principles within ethics, as there is no final proof of the Axiom of Uniformity by reference to other principles established within inductive science.

In the last section of <u>A System of Logic</u> (Gorovitz, p. 4), Mill explains the relation and difference between "Art" (which has ethics as its method) and "science", which leads to an explanation of the role of the first principles within each system:

> The art proposes to itself an end to be attained, defines the end, and hands it over to the science. The science receives it, considers it as a phenomenon or effect to be studied, and having investigated its causes and conditions, sends it back to art with a theorem of the combinations of circumstances by which it could be produced.

Art (and eventually, ethics) proposes ends and science (at least, in its pragmatic function) tells us how best to attain those ends. Thus, the first principle of ethics serves as the basis of justification of ends by giving us a ultimate criterion by which alternative ends can be assessed.

The Principle of Utility serves as the foundation of utilitarianism, an ethical theory, and is not identical to it, but Mill is not especially clear on this point. This is important, since to understand

THE PROOF OF THE THEORY

Mill's proof we need to be clear about exactly what he is trying to prove. In Chapter Two of <u>Utilitarianism</u> (p. 7), he writes:

> The creed which accepts as the foundation of morals "utility" or the "greatest happiness principle" holds that actions are right in proportion as they tend to promote happiness; wrong as they tend to produce the reverse of happiness.

But in Chapter Four of <u>Utilitarianism</u> (p. 34), the most important chapter in regard to the proof of the Principle of Utility, Mill writes:

> The utilitarian doctrine is that happiness is desirable, and the only thing desirable, as an end; all other things being only desirable as means to that end.

The difference between these two definitions is that the first depends on a chain of reasoning that is grounded on the second. Once it has been determined that only happiness is desirable as an end, then actions are right or wrong depending on the happiness and unhappiness they produce. Thus, it is only the principle in the second definition, that only happiness is desirable as an end, that serves as the foundation for utiltarianism, and is the counterpart of the Axiom of Uniformity.

How might we proceed to prove this principle, that only happiness is desirable as an end? Staying with the analogy with the system of inductive knowledge, if this is the foundational principle within the ethical theory then there can be no appeal to any other statement within ethics, since all other statements within Mill's ethics presuppose this principle. Like the Axiom of Uniformity, the Principle of Utility is a general hypothesis that is deemed the most reasonable hypothesis that might serve as the basis of ethics, and like the Axiom of Uniformity, this hypothesis is based upon observation and induction, as has been shown in the preceding chapter.

THE PROOF OF THE THEORY

I see the argument of the preceding paragraphs to be similar to the position put forth by E. W. Hall in "The "proof" of utility in Bentham and Mill" (p. 106). Hall writes:

> Mill makes use of two considerations... not to <u>prove</u> the principle of utility but to <u>make it acceptable</u> to reasonable men.

These two considerations are what Hall calls "intellectual honesty" and "psychological realism". The appeal to intellectual honesty is based upon an observation that in our day-to-day lives, we tacitly assume something similar to the Principle of Utility, so to remain honest, either we should alter our basic assumptions or our ethical theory ought to be consistent with them. A utilitarian takes the latter option and it is unlikely, on this view, that someone holding some other theory would actually alter his or her day-to-day life and the assumptions on which it is based.

Hall's discussion of "psychological realism" is the stronger of the two points. Inductive generalization is not open to empiricists as a method upon which to establish a first principle in ethics because we have no direct perception of ethical attributes (Hall disregards "moral sense" theory here). Just as it is nonsense to assert the existence of visible or audible entities that are never seen nor heard, if people did not regularly appeal to a proposed ethical standard then it would be nonsense to propose it to them.(37)

A problem with Hall's view is that it seems that there are ethical first principles other than the Principle of Utility that could pass these two tests of intellectual honesty and psychological realism. For example, Donagan's <u>The Theory of Morality</u> (pp. 66-68) describes a non-utilitarian theory based upon the intrinsic value of the person, and is a view that could

---

37. "The "proof" of utility in Bentham and Mill" by E. W. Hall, pp. 106-107 and pp. 114-115. Also see Wellman's "A Reinterpretation of Mill's Proof", p. 271, Popkin's "A Note on the "Proof" of Utility in J.S. Mill", and <u>Utilitarianism</u>, pp. 37-38.

THE PROOF OF THE THEORY

be adopted with intellectual honesty. Donagan's view also passes the psychological realism test in that there does exist a tendency to ethically justify actions with this sort of appeal. However, if we assume something like Mill's Psychological Hedonism then Donagan's theory will fail the second test. On this assumption, it makes no sense to found a system of ethics on anything other than the Principle of Utility because our ultimate desires are for happiness. To propose any other end of human action would be to propose an end contrary to our most basic desires, and so the proposal is doomed to fail.

The proof of the Principle of Utility given by Mill in the fourth chapter of Utilitarianism has the following general form:

1. Relative to each individual, his own happiness is desirable as an end to him (This is based on observation and psychological realism).

2. Relative to each individual, nothing but that which falls within his own concept of happiness can be desirable as an end to him (This follows from 1. and Mill's Psychological Hedonism).

3. There is something more desirable as an end, the overall happiness of the community, that supersedes the desirability of the happiness of any individual (This is Mill's composition argument which will be discussed shortly).

---

4. An action is right, and thus ought to be performed, if it results in the greatest overall happiness of the community (This assumes consequentialism).(38)

Careful observation of what people actually desire points to the first proposition in the proof. Each person desires his or her own happiness. As pointed out

---

38. My interpretation of the general form of the proof is similar to that given by Atkinson in "J.S. Mill's "Proof" of the Principle of Utility", pp. 161-162; by Kleinig in "The Fourth Chapter of Mill's Utilitarianism", p. 199; and by Hall in "The proof of utility in Bentham and Mill", pp.103-109.

THE PROOF OF THE THEORY

long ago by Aristotle (Nichomachean Ethics 1097b), happiness is not desired as a means to some other thing. Thus, at least, happiness is one thing that is known to be desired by people as an end. There are, of course, other things that can be observed as being desired, but are these things desired as ends or desired for the happiness that they are expected to produce? Mill considers the desire for virtue as an example. He writes:

> ...they [utilitarians] also recognize as a psychological fact the possibility of its [virtue] being, to the individual, a good in itself, without looking to any end beyond it...This opinion is not...a departure from the happiness principle. The ingredients of happiness are very various, and each of them is desirable in itself, and not merely when considered as swelling an aggregate.(Utilitarianism, p. 35)

This is an important passage. First, it proposes that the definition of happiness is relative to the individual. This seems opposed to the important competent judges passage in Chapter Two, which defines the higher pleasures, a definition that leads to the definition of happiness as including those pleasures found superior by the testimony of competent judges. Clearly, not everyone is a competent judge. Thus, some people's views on the nature of happiness will differ significantly from the testimony of competent judges, and it is likely that these people are mistaken.

Mill has been accused of equivocating on two senses of `desirable´ in his apparent move from the observation that only happiness is desired to the conclusion that only happiness is desirable, the sense of the latter meaning `ought to be desired´.(39) We have all been taught on our mother's knee (so the story goes)

---

39. G.E. Moore claims that Mill equivocates on "desirable" in Principia Ethica, p. 67. Carl Wellman disagrees. See "A Reinterpretation of Mill's Proof", p. 270.

THE PROOF OF THE THEORY

that just because we feel the desire for something, this does not make it desirable. If a youngster desires to cross the highway to visit a friend, the action might not really be desirable, because the youngster lacks an appreciation of the risk involved. The point of the criticism is that it seems that Mill is opposing one of the best known and most widely held ethical beliefs. Mill has made an error here, but the source of the error is not his lack of attention to the senses of the word `desirable´, and thus, is not an equivocation. His great error is being overcommitted to Psychological Determinism and Psychological Hedonism. If we grant Mill these theories then his move from `the desired´ to `the desirable´ is justified, assuming the "ought implies can" principle. As I have have already argued, a more plausible and liberal view is that, on their own merit, we are free to choose and realize the higher pleasures and superior lifestyles that encourage the experience of the higher pleasures.

The next stage of Mill´s proof moves from the second proposition, that only happiness is desirable (or is of intrinsic moral value) to each individual, to the conclusion that there is a greater overall good, the greatest happiness for the community. For such an important point, he has little to say:

> ...each person´s happiness is a good to that person, and the general happiness, therefore, a good to the aggregate of all persons. (<u>Utilitarianism</u>, p. 34)

On this point, Mill has been accused of committing the fallacy of composition.(40) Even if it be granted that there is `the good´ defined individually, there seems little evidence to support the conclusion that there exists a more general good defined as the greatest overall happiness within the community. It seems possible that there is `the good´ of each individual, but that there is no solid basis for `the good´ of the community. Mill is claiming that from the perspective

---

40. G.E. Moore holds that Mill´s reasoning actually leads to egoism rather than utilitarianism. See <u>Principia Ethica</u>, p. 104.

THE PROOF OF THE THEORY

of the group the overall happiness of the group is a good to it in a way parallel to the individual's good being good to him from his limited perspective. But, why is not the good of the king (or some other minority) the overall good, taken from the larger perspective? I see no fallacy in assuming that, relative to the individual, his own happiness is the good for him, but that from the larger perspective, the overall good is the happiness of the king. The missing premise is the assumption that (approximately) the happiness of any one individual is as valuable as the happiness of any other. In an ant colony, the "happiness" of the queen is paramount, and the "happiness" of the workers means little in comparison. In a democracy, we are all (approximately) equal in status, and so the happiness of each citizen is given equal weight. This stage of Mill's proof assumes this democratic principle.

If Mill meant his conclusion to follow without any other additional implied premise then there is a gap in his reasoning (41) for as F.H. Bradley writes in Ethical Studies (p. 113):

> If many pigs are fed at one trough, each desires his own food, and somehow as a consequence does seem to desire the food of all; and by parity of reasoning it should follow that each pig, desiring his own pleasure, desires also the pleasure of all. But as this scarcely seems conformable to experience, I suppose there must be something wrong with the argument...

What is wrong is that each pig desires food and

---

41. In "Fallacies in and about Mill's Utilitarianism", p. 349, Raphael quotes from a 1868 Mill letter as follows: "I did not mean that every human being's happiness is a good to every other human being; though I think in a good state of society and education it would be so. I merely meant in this particular sentence to argue that since A's happiness is a good, B's a good, C's a good, &c., the sum of all these goods must be a good."

pleasure of eating it for himself. To desire porky´s slop is to desire to have porky´s slop for yourself, but to desire porky´s pleasure is to desire pleasure for porky, not for yourself.

I agree that it is reasonable to adopt this position, that the good of the community is superior to the good of the individual, and in fact, this is my own view. However, I disagree that there is a proof that may be given in support of it to the point of proving that an ethical egoist or elitist has committed an error. If, initially, `the good´ is defined relative to the individual then one method by which the conflicts that will eventually arise could be settled is to hold that the overall good of the group be put above the desires of individuals. What I am saying is that there are no a priori grounds for this inference. An ethical egoist is being dishonest by placing his personal desires over the desires of others. Ethical egoists are deceiving themselves if they believe that their own desires and status are intrinsically more valuable than the desires and status of others, but this is hardly a proof.

The final stage of Mill´s proof is the move from adopting the greatest overall benefits for the community as being the greatest good to holding that actions are right if and only if they produce the greatest overall good to the community. As explained in the first chapter of this essay, this move is not as simple as merely following from the definition of a right action, and instead assumes consequentialism.

3. UTILITARIANISM AND THE INDIVIDUAL

There are several connected objections to utilitarian theories that are based upon the idea that utilitarianism is an impersonal theory that neglects the importance of persons taken as individuals. Examples that illustrate this point are apparent injustices in cases in which the rights of a minority are violated in order to achieve the greatest happiness for the majority. These are seen as violations of basic liberties. Utilitarianism seems in some cases to prescribe actions most people would find highly immoral. For example, if there are currently 250 million people in the U.S.A. and if we assume that the current average level of happiness is a `4´ then as a

UTILITARIANISM AND THE INDIVIDUAL

base we have 1.000 billion hedonic units. Now, suppose that it was proposed that 10% of the population be enslaved and assigned the most disagreeable tasks within the society. These slaves would wash the dishes, dig the ditches, pick the fruit, and sweep the streets. The slaves would not necessarily be selected on the basis of skin color or national origin, but, perhaps, by a lottery or better, by some utilitarian criterion of suitability. It is reasonable to suppose that the happiness of the majority would be increased to an average level of 5 hedonic units, and that the happiness of the enslaved minority would decrease to an average level of 2 hedonic units. There might be some feelings of guilt on the part of the majority that would bring down their average, but, I think, the overall average would increase on account of the pleasure received by being relieved of these unpleasant tasks. The enslaved minority need not be miserable. They could be housed in fairly comfortable barracks and given a wholesome, but plain, diet. Multiplying the resulting 5 average hedonic units by the 225 million in the majority yields 1.125 billion hedonic units, and 2 units times 25 million slaves equals 50 million units, with an overall sum of 1.175 billion units, clearly a great advantage over the base 1.000 billion hedonic units. Therefore, applying utilitarianism to the problem seems to prescribe the enslavement of a minority. This seems absurd, and thus indicates a flaw in the utilitarian theory.

To deal with this objection, let us consider the relation of the views put forth in Mill´s other important essay, On Liberty to those put forth in Utilitarianism. On Liberty was first published in 1859, two years prior to the initial publication of Utilitarianism. A discussion of the relation between these two works involves the more general issue of the comparison of utilitarianism, a doctrine oriented to the needs of the society, to libertarianism, a doctrine which puts more emphasis on rights of the individual. On Liberty contains forceful arguments in favor of individual rights and freedoms. If I can demonstrate that the doctrines proposed in On Liberty are consistent with the utilitarianism of Mill´s Utilitarianism then great progress will have been made in alleviating the above objections.

UTILITARIANISM AND THE INDIVIDUAL

The views put forth in On Liberty are based upon the Harm Principle, which is the basic principle of libertarianism. In On Liberty (p. 9), Mill writes:

> The object of this essay is to assert one very simple principle...That the only purpose for which power can be rightfully exercised over any member of a civilized community, against his will, is to prevent harm to others.

A question immediately arises. Is the Harm Principle consistent with the Principle of Utility? If the answer to this question is no, then it appears that within two years Mill published two essays, each putting forth a theory that contradicts the other.

Clearly, the Principle of Utility and the Harm Principle, as above defined, are inconsistent. There certainly are cases in which greater overall benefits are produced by exercising power over an individual against his will, even though he is harming no one. Examples that show this inconsistency are examples in which the happiness produced by forcing an individual to act in a particular way outweigh the unhappiness produced by that action. For example, in a state of national emergency it might well follow from the Principle of Utility that the military draft be reinstated, because the overall benefits produced by the increased protection of the society outweigh the unhappiness caused by some people being forced to enter the military against their will. People who choose to be unemployed and who also have job skills that are in great demand are not harming others, as usually understood in the application of the Harm Principle. If they were forced to work against their will then, at least in some cases, more overall benefits would accrue than harm. For example, there are some medical researchers who have lost interest and have voluntarily chosen not to pursue their research. There certainly are several cases within this category such that if these people were forced to return to their research then there would be some advancement that would be beneficial to mankind. In these cases, it would be right according to the Principle of Utility to force these people to continue their work, but it would be wrong to do so according to the Harm Principle, and thus, the two theories are inconsistent.

UTILITARIANISM AND THE INDIVIDUAL

Another important area is the freedom of expression. No doubt, there are many cases in which granting freedom of expression provides overall benefits to the society, but surely there are plenty of cases in which this is not so. In some cases, granting the freedom of expression disturbs the individuals to which an opinion is directed, and this outweighs the benefits that occur as a result of granting the freedom of expression. An example might well be allowing members of religious cults to express their views in public places, such as airports. The benefits from allowing this practice are minimal. Those within the cult who wish to see their organization prosper benefit from this freedom. I don´t think that the members who are required to proselytize benefit much from this activity. The majority of people to which these advances are directed would be happier if the expression of these opinions were disallowed. The occasional winning of a convert is rarely a benefit to society or the convert. There are probably some cases in which the convert would have led a life of crime instead of joining the cult, and so, in these cases, there would be some benefit to society.

It is likely that the curtailment of the rights of expression of Neo-Nazi organizations would be beneficial to society. There is currently a group in northern Idaho that is promoting the idea of excluding Afro-Americans, Jews, and other minorities from the area. Bombings and counterfeiting have taken place as a result of this rhetoric. The only benefits that result from this freedom of expression are the happiness of the very small number of persons in this group and those in sympathy with their cause.

The solution to this apparent inconsistency is that Mill is really not a true libertarian, a true libertarian being someone who holds that individual rights ought to be upheld even if the practice produces less than optimum benefits for the society. Rather, Mill is arguing that adopting the practice that certain kinds of freedom be allowed will result in overall benefits for society. In other words, Mill´s apparently libertarian views put forth in On Liberty are really based upon utilitarianism. If this interpretation is correct, and if Mill is right about the implications of this version of utilitarianism, then utilitarianism is really a much more attractive view in regard to basic freedoms and rights than often supposed. The views put forth in *On Liberty* are a proposal that each civilized society grant each adult citizen full rights of freedom of expression, freedom of lifestyle, and freedom of association.

The first bit of textual evidence in support of this interpretation comes from the page following the definition of the Harm Principle. It reads:

> It is proper to state that I forego any advantage which could be derived to my argument from the idea of abstract right as a thing independent of utility. I regard utility as the ultimate appeal on all ethical questions; but it must be utility in the largest sense, grounded on the permanent interests of man as a progressive being.(*On Liberty*, p. 10)

This is a perfectly straightforward statement in support of the interpretation I have given. Mill is not arguing for the Harm Principle on any abstract grounds, but instead is claiming that utilitarian arguments are sufficient to support the Harm Principle.

Further evidence for this interpretation is the way Mill argues for these freedoms. Each of his arguments is thoroughly utilitarian, showing the benefits of adopting the practice of granting the freedoms of expression, lifestyle, and association. That Mill only argues for these three types of freedom is itself evidence that his argument is based on utilitarianism, since he neglects the myriad of other freedoms that might be based upon the Harm Principle. There are also exceptions to these freedoms. They do not apply to children nor do they apply to "backward stages of society". (*On Liberty*, pp. 9-10) These exceptions, no doubt, have their basis in utilitarianism.

The arguments given in Chapter II of *On Liberty* (pp. 16-33) in favor of the freedom of expression uphold the above interpretation. Mill spends several paragraphs discussing human infallibility. If some humans were infallible then, perhaps, some cases of censorship would be justified. But, Mill argues, no humans are infallible, so there is no guarantee that falsehoods would not be guarded by censorship. Society

UTILITARIANISM AND THE INDIVIDUAL

benefits when falsehoods are bared and corrected. Therefore, universal freedom of expression should be granted to adult citizens of advanced civilizations. This is clearly a utilitarian argument.

The next argument for granting freedom of expression begins by making a distinction between views generally held by a society that are correct, incorrect, and mixed. If the view generally held within a particular society is correct, Mill argues that the society still benefits from freedom of expression because freedom of expression allows for the members of the society to use the arguments given in support of some mistaken view as a foil by which the value of their position can be fully appreciatied. Besides, if a society had a full and correct set of beliefs, to disallow freedom of expression is not conducive to the mental health of the society. Knowledge is not the mere reiteration of the received views within a society, but instead requires appreciation of the opposing point of view, and allowing freedom of expression is the best way by which the opposing point of view may be put forth.

More likely, there are some mistaken views that are generally held within the society. It is generally true that a society is harmed by its citizens holding false opinions. Believing that the world is flat impedes progress in developing world travel and trade. Believing that women are inferior and unable to handle responsibility deprives the society of the talents of half of its citizens. Mill´s most ingenious argument is directed towards the case in which the society does hold the correct view. People are more inclined to believe that freedom of expression is harmful in cases in which the correct opinion is held. If the view generally held by society is mistaken, though it is unusual that citizens are aware of such shortcomings, then the citizens are harmed by disallowing freedom of expression because freedom of expression affords the opportunity to exchange ideas and eventually correct mistaken opinions. Similarly, on the third and most likely possibility, that generally held views are partially mistaken, granting freedom of expression allows for the improvement of those views and the social progress that follows. Thus, the manner in which Mill argues for freedom of expression is utilitarian.

UTILITARIANISM AND THE INDIVIDUAL

An examination of Mill's arguments for freedom of lifestyle in the third chapter of On Liberty yields a similar result. There he argues that people should be granted freedom of lifestyle because the benefits by doing so outweighs the harm, the main benefits being providing an environment conducive to mental health and the development of genius. Freedom of lifestyle also complements the freedom of expression, because without the freedom to act on ideas there is little value in having the freedom to express them. Thus, these are also utilitarian arguments.

The third area of textual evidence that can be given in support of the interpretation that the theory in On Liberty is consistent with utilitarianism is the argument given for exceptions to the practice of allowing these freedoms of expression, lifestyle, and association. Interference will be allowed under the following conditions:

> There is no question here about restricting individuality, or impeding the trial of new and original experiments in living. The things it is sought to prevent are things which have been tried and condemned from the beginning of the world until now...
> (On Liberty, p. 79)

Examples Mill gives are "gambling", "drunkenness", "incontinence", "idleness", and "uncleanliness" (p. 78). The idea is that if experience has shown time after time that a type of activity is harmful to the individual, then interference is justified, since it is unreasonable to expect that these activities will be beneficial to the individual or to the society in which he or she lives. In other words, if there are incontestable utilitarian grounds for interference then the freedoms granted by the Harm Principle are overturned. Mill's general thesis put forth in On Liberty is that when in doubt the good of both society and the individual are best served by allowing the greatest amount of freedom possible. But, if it is clear that interference will benefit the individual and society then interference is justified. The radical libertarian view is that utilitarian considerations are irrelevant to these questions, and that freedom should be allowed even when it is regularly harmful to the individual or society. Mill relies on utilitarian considerations, and therefore, his view is not radical libertarianism.

By the arguments given in On Liberty, it is shown that utilitarianism need not be a doctrine that rides roughshod over individual rights. Mill has given us a convincing statement that proposes extending individual rights far beyond the norms of the nineteenth century. Yet, Mill´s arguments seem insufficient to answer objections like the enslavement example given earlier. These examples run counter to the main thesis of On Liberty, that there is utility in granting freedoms and individual rights. My reply, which I see as an extension of Mill´s theory, is that these sorts of examples can be handled when Qualitative Utilitarianism is applied at the most general level, which is the subject of the following section.

4. PRACTICAL IMPLICATIONS OF THE THEORY

The practical implications of Qualitative Utilitarianism are that we ought to foster the enjoyment of the higher pleasures, as determined by the experience of competent judges. This amounts to nothing short of a massive program for social reform. There are two main aims within this program, one negative and one positive. The negative aim is the elimination of poverty, disease, and the other sources of human suffering. In these areas, the practical implications of the quantitative and qualitative theories are quite similar. It is in the area of the positive aim that the two theories differ. In Chapter Three, I have described the unsavory practical implications of Quantitative Utilitarianism. The practical implications of Qualitative Utilitarianism call for the establishment of educational facilities, libraries, art museums, centers for the performing arts, and national parks. The enjoyment of the higher pleasures does not require great monetary wealth, but extreme poverty, disease, and malnutrition all preclude the enjoyment of higher pleasures, and so, their elimination is a necessary condition that must first be met before the full enjoyment of the higher pleasures is possible.

It is here that the enslavement problem reenters the discussion. There are three possible situations in which the problem is cast, depending on the economics

PRACTICAL IMPLICATIONS OF THE THEORY

of the society. Either it is possible that an environment be created that allows for all of the citizens to enjoy the higher pleasures, or it is only possible for the majority of the citizens to enjoy the higher pleasures, or thirdly, it is only possible for a minority to enjoy the higher pleasures. Within Qualitative Utilitarianism, enslavement (and, presumably, the lack of an opportunity to enjoy the higher pleasures) is not acceptable as a permanent social structure. But if it were true that enslavement of some citizens (or at least, taking away from them the opportunity to enjoy the higher pleasures, which, in this context, amounts to the same thing) was necessary to produce an environment in which some other citizens are provided the opportunity to enjoy the higher pleasures, then this is justified. The best educated and most intellectually gifted citizens are the obvious candidates for being within this elite class. In most Western democracies, it is possible to provide education and a suitable environment to the large majority of citizens so that they may come to enjoy the higher pleasures. In other societies, it may only be possible to provide this opportunity to a few, selected citizens. Keeping in mind that the duty still exists to work to extend these privileges to all citizens. Enslavement, in such a case, is not wrong according to Qualitative Utilitarianism.

The second positive aim prescribed by Qualitative Utilitarianism is to create an environment that stimulates and encourages the enjoyment of higher pleasures. Consider the example of higher pleasures of the enjoyment of literature. Before the enjoyment of the pleasures of reading great literature is possible, one must be educated to the point of being able to read the language in which the literature is produced. Further instruction in literature might foster the appreciation of literature. The most efficient way to teach the masses how to appreciate literature is through the establishment of a public education system. Public libraries provide access to great works of literature, and so, is also important in creating an environment in which the pleasures of the appreciation of literature will likely occur. Art museums are places where great works of Art are displayed so that the public may enjoy them. Likewise, centers for the performing arts allow for the public to experience operas, symphonies, and dance. I include national parks

PRACTICAL IMPLICATIONS OF THE THEORY

with the preceding activities, because within this line of thinking, since they can be seen as centers for the enjoyment of the higher pleasures of the appreciation of the beauty of nature.

It has been 125 years since the initial publication of <u>Utilitarianism</u>. In that time, there has been much progress in western Europe and North America along the lines prescibed by Qualitative Utilitarianism. There has been progress in the elimination of disease and poverty and there has been progress in establishing public education and centers in which the public may experience the pleasures of literature, Art, and nature. Although I am sure that the publication of Mill´s theory is not directly responsible for this progress, I do think that his theory is a statement and formulation of the liberal spirit of progressive thinkers in the nineteenth century, and that this movement is to a great degree responsible for what social progress has been made in the last 125 years. In short, many of the finest accomplishments of mankind in the past 125 years match the prescriptions of Mill´s theory and that is a powerful confirmation of the theory.

In regard to what I call the "life and death" issues, the application of Qualitative Utilitarianism yields results similar to those of the application of other forms of utilitarianism. Abortion, contraception, and euthanasia are acceptable insofar as they produce a greater balance of happiness over what harm comes from them. Qualitative Utilitarianism provides especially interesting insights into cases in which individuals are rendered incapable of happiness as defined by the theory as a life that necessarily includes the enjoyment of the higher pleasures. If faced with the choice of spending tax dollars on prolonging the life of people injured by illness or accident to the point of being no longer capable of attaining happiness or spending tax dollars on education, clearly we should opt for education.

One might object that Mill´s theory has a prejudice for the values of aristocratic Victorian society, In other words, it unjustifiably values the life of an English gentleman over some other equally desirable lifestyle. There are really three separate questions to be answered here. Is Mill´s method of evaluation prejudiced towards the values of the Victorian minority or is it in the application of his method that the prejudice arises? Or, thirdly, is there really a prejudice towards these values at all? There is nothing in Mill's method of evaluation that incorporates this alleged prejudice. The appeal to the experience of competent judges can be made outside of Victorian society, and would yield results in other cultures similar to those imagined by Mill, placing a high value on the enjoyment of literature, Art, and nature as previously set out. I would add to the list the pleasures of friendship, marital love and raising a family, pleasures that are not included in Mill's list, but the list is not represented by Mill as being final and complete. Pleasures associated with intellectual development are those which Mill most often mentions as being of the higher sort, and these are pleasures that might be easily seen as having a prejudicial element, since one might think they have not historically been so valued in cultures outside of Europe. But this is not so. In almost every case, when the appreciation of literature and Art has extended beyond the inner circles of the aristocracy and priesthood, it has come to have been held in high esteem. In the history of the Chinese, Japanese, Hindu, and Arabic cultures, the appreciation of literature and the Arts followed the education of the middle classes. Today, these values are still held in high esteem in every progressive society. The life of an English gentleman is really only an example of the life of a person who has had the education and opportunity to experience what Mill finds to be the higher pleasures. The same holds for the Chinese gentleman, the Japanese gentleman, the Hindu gentleman, and the Arabic gentleman.

5. CONCLUDING REMARKS

When properly set out and explained, Qualitative Utilitarianism is a defensible and attractive theory that deserves a more thoughtful reception than that which it has so often received. I am not claiming to have solved all of the problems inherent within the theory, but I do claim to have presented the theory in a clearer and more defensible form than has been done before.

CONCLUDING REMARKS

John Stuart Mill wrote <u>Utilitarianism</u> as part of a project to blend utilitarianism with the humanistic tradition that reaches back to Plato and Aristotle. I see this essay as being an extension and refinement of that project. As we enter the next century (and millenium), our world will undoubtably become more complicated and the rhetoric addressed to how we should proceed will become more sophisticated and confusing. Qualitative Utilitarianism offers good prospects for providing clarification of these issues.

BIBLIOGRAPHY

Aristotle. Nicomachean Ethics (c.330 B.C.) (Martin Oswald, trans). (Indianapolis: The Library of Liberal Arts, 1962).

Bentham, Jeremy. An Introduction to the Principles of Morals and Legislation (1780). Reprinted in part in A Bentham Reader (Mary Peter Mack, ed.). (New York: Pegasus, 1969), pp. 78-144.

Berger, Fred R. Happiness, Justice, and Freedom. (Berkelely: U. of California Press, 1984).

Bradley, F.H. Ethical Studies (1876) (2nd ed.). (Oxford: Clarendon Press, 1927).

Bradley, Raymond, and Swartz, Norman. Possible Worlds. (Indianapolis: Hackett, 1979).

Brink, David O., "Utilitarian Morality and the Personal Point of View" in The Journal of Philosophy. Vol. LXXXIII, No. 8 (1986), pp. 417-438.

Broad, C.D. Five Types of Ethical Theory. (London: Routledge, 1930).

Butchvarov, P. "That Simple, Indefinable, Nonnatural Property Good", in Review of Metaphysics. Vol. XXX, No. 1 (1982), pp. 51-75.

Cohen, Elliot David. "J.S. Mill's Qualitative Hedonism: A Textual Analysis", in The Southern Journal of Philosophy. Vol. XVIII, No. 2 (1980).

Donagan, Alan. The Theory of Morality. (Chicago: U. of Chicago Press, 1977).

Edwards, Rem. Pleasures and Pains. (Ithaca, N.Y.: Cornell U. Press, 1979).

Ewing, A.C. "A Suggested Non-Naturalistic Analysis of Good" (1939), in Readings in Ethical Theory (Sellars and Hospers, eds.). (New York City: Appleton-Century-Crofts), pp. 115-129.

Feagin, Susan L. "Mill and Edwards on the Higher Pleasures", in Philosophy 58. (1983), pp. 244-252.

BIBLIOGRAPHY

Gibbs, Benjamin. "Higher and Lower Pleasures", in Philosophy 61. (1986), pp. 31-59.

Gorovitz, Samuel (ed.). Mill: Utilitarianism with Critical Essays. (Indianapolis: Bobbs-Merrill, 1971).

Gosling, J.C.B. Pleasure and Desire. (Oxford: Clarendon Press, 1969).

Hall, Everett W. "The "proof" of utility in Bentham and Mill" (1949), in Mill: Utilitarianism with Critical Essays (Samuel Gorovitz, ed.), pp. 99-116.

Hospers, John. Human Conduct. (New York: Harcourt Brace, 1961).

Kleinig, John. "The Fourth Chapter of Mill's Utilitarianism", in Australian Journal of Philosophy. Vol. 48, No. 2 (1970), pp. 197-295.

Kupperman, Joel J. "Vulgar Consequentialism", in Mind. Vol. LXXXIX (1980), pp. 321-337.

Leibniz, Gottfried. "Monadology" (1714). in Leibniz (G.R. Montgomery, trans.). (LaSalle, Illinois: Open Court, 1980).

Lyons, David. Forms and Limits of Utilitarianism. (Oxford: Clarendon Press, 1965).

McCloskey, H.J. "A Non-Utilitarian Approach to Punishment" (1965). Reprinted in Contemporary Utilitarianism (Michael D. Bayles, ed.). (Garden City, N.Y.: Anchor Books, 1968), pp. 239-259.

Mill, John Stuart. A System of Logic (1843). (London: Routledge, undated).

_____. On Liberty (1859). (Indianapolis: Hackett, 1978).

_____. Utilitarianism (1861). (Indianapolis: Hackett, 1979).

_____. Autobiography of John Stuart Mill (1873). (New York: Columbia U. Press, 1924).

BIBLIOGRAPHY

Moore, G.E. *Principia Ethica* (1903).
(Cambridge: Cambridge U. Press, 1966).

_____ *Ethics*.
(London: Oxford U. Press, 1912).

Narveson, Jan. *Morality and Utility*.
(Baltimore: Johns Hopkins, 1967).

Penelhum, Terence. "The Logic of Pleasure", in *Philosophy and Phenomenological Research*. Vol. XVII, No. 4 (1957), pp. 488-503.

Plato. *Collected Dialogues* (c.390 B.C.) (Hamilton and Cairns, eds.). (Princeton, N.J.: Princeton U. Press, 1961).

Popkin, Richard H. "A Note on the "Proof" of Utility in J.S. Mill", in *Ethics*. Vol. LXI, No. 1 (1950), pp. 66-68.

Quinn, Warren S. "Pleasure---Disposition or Episode", in *Philosophy and Phenomenological Research*. Vol. XXVIII, No. 4 (1968), pp. 578-586.

Quinton, Anthony. *Utilitarian Ethics*.
(London: Macmillan, 1973).

Raphael, D. Daiches. "Fallacies in and about Mill´s Utilitarianism", in *Philosophy*. Vol. XXX, No. 115 (1955), pp. 344-357.

Rawls, John. *A Theory of Justice*.
(Cambridge, MA: Harvard U. Press, 1971).

Regan, Donald. *Utilitarianism and Co-operation*.
(Oxford: Clarendon Press, 1980).

Ross, W. David. *Foundations of Ethics*.
(Oxford: Clarendon Press, 1939).

Ryle, Gilbert. *The Concept of Mind*.
(New York: Barnes and Noble, 1949).

_____ *Dilemmas*.
(Cambridge: Cambridge U. Press, 1954).

BIBLIOGRAPHY

Sartre, Jean-Paul. "Existentialism is a Humanism", in Existentialism and Human Emotions. (New York: Philosophical Library, 1957), pp. 9-51.

Sidgwick, Henry. The Methods of Ethics (1874) (7th ed). (Indianapolis: Hackett, 1981).

Smart, J.J.C. "Extreme and Restricted Utilitarianism" (1956), Reprinted in Theories of Ethics (P. Foot, ed.). (London: Oxford U. Press, 1967), pp. 171-183.

──────────── "An outline of a system of utilitarian ethics" (1961), in Utilitarianism: For and Against. (Cambridge: Cambridge U. Press, 1973), pp. 3-74.

Sobel, Jordan Howard. "Rule-utilitarianism", in Australian Journal of Philosophy. Vol. 46, No. 2 (1968).

Sosa, Ernest. "Mill´s Utilitarianism", in Mill´s Utiltarianism (Smith and Sosa, eds.). (Belmont, CA: Wadsworth, 1969), pp. 154-172.

Stubbs, Anne. "The Pros and Cons of Consequentialism", in Philosophy 56. (1981), pp. 497-516.

Wellman, Carl. "A Reinterpretation of Mill´s Proof", in Ethics. Vol. LXIX, No. 4 (1959), pp. 268-276.

Williams, Bernard. "A critique of utilitarianism", in Utilitarianism: for and against. (Cambridge: Cambridge U. Press, 1973), pp. 75-150.

Wilson, Fred. "Mill´s Proof that Happiness is the Criterion of Morality", in Journal of Business Ethics 1. (1982), pp. 59-72.

Wittgenstein, Ludwig. Philosophical Investigations (1953) (3rd ed.) (G.E.M. Anscombe, trans.). (Oxford: Basil Blackwell, 1958).

INDEX

Aristotle

    values intellectual pleasures, 1.
    definition of voluntary action, 44.

Bentham, Jeremy

    a psychological hedonist, 54.
    hedonistic calculus, 72-74.

Bradley, F.H.

    qualitative hedonism is inconsistent, 84.
    on Mill's composition argument, 120-121.

Brandt, Richard

    on irrational desires, 64.

Broad, C.D.

    "tripartite division" of the mind, 58.

Consequentialism

    definition of, 5.
    true by definition?, 13-14.
    and responsibility, 17-19.
    ambiguity in, 24-26.
    objections to, 33-34.
    paradox of, 34-36.

Donagan, Alan

    not confused about the meaning of `right', 13.
    discusses voter's paradox, 31.
    objects to consequentialism, 33-36.

Edwards, Rem

    pleasure is not simply behavior, 55.
    interpretation of Mill on pleasure, 98.
    on ethical pluralism, 102.
    on the location of pleasures and pains, 104-105.

Freedom (Free Will)

    assumptions made by, 20.

INDEX

General Consequentialism

    definition of, 27-30.
    compared to Utilitarian Generalization, 32-34.

Gosling, J.C.B.

    definition of hedonism, 45.
    definition of pleasure, 92.

Hall, E.W.

    on Mill's "proof" of utilitarianism, 116-117.

Hedonism

    definition of, 41.
    and Humanism, 41-44.
    Psychological Hedonism, 45-50.
    Ethical Hedonism, 51-55.

Kupperman, Joel J.

    on lack of arguments for consequentialism, 15.
    on the paradox of consequentialism, 35.

Lyons, David

    on utilitarian generalization, 32-33.
    defines act and rule utilitarianism, 37.
    orange picker example, 38.

Mill, John Stuart

    defines utilitarianism, 1.
    defines qualitative hedonism, 81-83, 102-104.
    first and foremost Qualitative Utilitarian, 3-4.
    argument for consequentialism, 15-16.
    action is separate from motivation, 15-17.
    a psychological hedonist, 46.
    "social feelings" as motivation, 48.
    "standard of morals" not "rule of action", 49.
    influenced by European humanists, 50.
    on objections to hedonism, 74.
    arguments for qualitative hedonism, 91-100.
    on pleasure and happiness, 98, 105-107.

INDEX

Mill, John Stuart (continued)

>defines pleasure, 98.
examples of higher pleasures, 102.
the "proof" of utilitarianism, 111-121.
libertarianism based on utilitarianism, 122-128.
his ethics has a Victorian bias?, 130-131.

Moore, G.E.

>argument for consequentialism, 13-14.
`good´ is a simple concept, 14.
definition of hedonism, 42.
qualitative hedonism is inconsistent, 83-85.
definition of pleasure, 86-88.
Principle of Organic Unity, 93-94.
claims Mill equivocates `desirable´, 118.
on Mill´s composition argument, 119.

Narveson, Jan

>definition of utilitarianism, 2.
definition of pleasure, 63.

"Ought Implies Can" principle

>definiton of, 52.

Penelhum, Terence

>definition of pleasure, 55.
definition of dispositional concept, 56.
on false pleasures, 57.

Plato

>values intellectual pleasures, 1.
on false pleasures, 57.
on the trading places argument, 95.
on the competent judges argument, 97.

Pleasure

>Sensation theory of, 59-60, 87-90.
Desire theory of, 62-66, 88-90.
Happiness and, 105-107.

INDEX

Possible Worlds

   necessary for ethics, 20-21.
   model for decision theory, 24-25.

Qualitative Hedonism

   definition of, 81-83, 109-111.
   alleged inconsistency of, 83-88.
   higher capacity argument for, 90-92.
   trading places argument for, 95-96.
   competent judges argument for, 96-100.
   pluralistic variety of, 101-104.

Qualitative utilitarianism

   definition of, 3.
   practical implications of, 77-78, 128-131.
   empiricism and, 93-94.

Quantitative Hedonism

   definition of, 69.

Quantitative Utilitarianism

   practical implications of, 74-80.
   Pleasure Center Intepretation, 75-80.

Rawls, John

   on the competent judges argument, 100.
   on "risk", 100-101.

Ross, W.D.

   `ought´ limited to exertion, 19.

Ryle, Gilbert

   definition of pleasure, 55.
   on the location of pleasures and pains, 105.

Sidgwick, Henry

   definition of utilitarianism, 2.
   definition of pleasure, 58, 89-90.
   qualitative hedonism is inconsistent, 83-84.

INDEX

Smart, J.J.C.

    Possible Worlds and ethics, 21.
    practical implications of utilitarianism, 79-80.

Stubbs, Anne

    definition of consequentialism, 6.
    embezzlement example, 8-9.
    cowardly soldier example, 10-13.
    "rational standards" in ethics, 19.
    on act and rule utilitarianism, 39.

Utilitarianism

    definition of, 1-2.
    act and rule, 36-39.
    proof of, 111-120.
    and individual rights, 121-128.

Wittgenstein, Ludwig

    on "family resemblance", 88.